Advance Praise for *Solid Ground*

"In telling his personal story, Tom Lewis has provided a road map for a richer, more meaningful, and happier life. Take that road!"
—**Dennis Prager, Author and Syndicated Talk Show Host**

"More wisdom than a college education."
—**Charlie Kirk, Founder and CEO of Turning Point USA**

"Tom Lewis has written an invaluable book that should be required reading for everyone who wants to live the American Dream."
—**Mike Pence, 48th Vice President of the United States**

"What *Solid Ground* offers is a return to the timeless fundamentals of success and happiness and the keys to building a happy and healthy life. It is a book that gives insight into *how* to live, not just how to make a living. Its messages are profound and empowering."
—**Robert Kiyosaki, Author of *Rich Dad Poor Dad***

"Solid advice from a solid guy. This book is the *grounding* that so many want and need. If you wish to get your feet under you—and get going on the life you've dreamed of—then start by reading this book."
—**Meg Jay, PhD, Author of *The Defining Decade***

T0361624

SOLID GROUND

T.W. LEWIS

A POST HILL PRESS BOOK
ISBN: 979-8-88845-904-1
ISBN (eBook): 979-8-88845-905-8

Solid Ground:
Ten Proven Principles for Success
© 2020, 2023, 2024 by T.W. Lewis
All Rights Reserved

Post Hill Press
New York • Nashville
posthillpress.com

Published in the United States of America
1 2 3 4 5 6 7 8 9 10

For every young adult in America
who wants to find success and happiness.

TABLE OF CONTENTS

PART IV: LIFE'S GREATEST ACHIEVEMENTS

PART V: INSPIRATION FOR THE SOUL

FOREWORD

"Your future is created by what you do today,
not tomorrow."

—Robert Kiyosaki

Tom Lewis and I crossed paths a few years back in a memorable way. I'll share the story with you here because I believe it shows why the ideas in this book are so important today—and why Tom is just the man to deliver them.

In early 2022, I was invited to speak at an event at Arizona State University hosted by the T.W. Lewis Center for Personal Development, a center Tom had created through his philanthropy. I knew Tom a little, and I admired his vision for the Lewis Center. It aimed to supplement the classroom education that colleges offer with the kind of practical life advice and experience students almost never receive. Advice like how to prepare for a job interview, balance a budget, or buy a car. Anyone who's read my book *Rich Dad Poor Dad* knows that kind of practical education, grounded in a solid foundation of financial education, is very close to my heart. And I have long questioned educators—at all levels—related to why financial education is so seldom taught in schools. Long ago I decided that we needed to look, and operate, outside the traditional education system, to offer students the multifaceted and real-world education they need. The T.W. Lewis Center was this kind of initiative.

One of the Lewis Center's programs was a speaker series that brought in successful professionals from many different backgrounds to talk about careers and real life. When the folks at the center reached out to me to see if I would participate, I suggested an event titled "Health, Wealth, and Happiness." I wanted to share with students what I'd learned over the years about the pursuit of these great goals and how intertwined they were. I also wanted to invite Dennis Prager, whose advice on happiness has had a profound effect on me... as it has on Tom. Later we added a third speaker, Charlie Kirk of Turning Point USA.

My instinct was correct, and we found that "Health, Wealth, and Happiness" was a topic students were eager to explore. We spoke to a packed house in the biggest theatre at ASU—there were nearly 1500 students and young adults in attendance. The overall messages aligned with what you'll find in *Solid Ground*... the importance of faith, family, and financial education as key components for a rich life as well as the idea that each person must take responsibility for his or her own success and happiness.

The young people in the audience that evening were hungry for these messages. But our presentation was not welcomed by all. Prior to the event, a vocal group of faculty and administrators worked together to fuel outrage, largely over the fact that both Prager and Kirk are outspoken conservatives. It seems our goal of offering a variety of voices and points of view was not embraced by the establishment and the very foundations of freedom of speech and freedom of expression were put to the test.

Whatever the case may have been, the fallout from the controversy— and the university's unwillingness to defend the Lewis Center—led to Tom canceling his gift to ASU and its closure that June. Imagine: A center, dedicated to sharing ideas and experiences, being shut down just because the "wrong" people shared their thoughts about health, wealth, and happiness. And a forum for learning—where all points of view should be entertained and respected—is no more. It was a sad and sobering day and a statement on the value we put on freedom of speech and expression. It's a tremendous loss for our country when ideology takes the place of practical wisdom.

It's against the backdrop of this controversy and the closing of the Lewis Center that I applaud this new edition of *Solid Ground*. In this book,

SOLID GROUND

Tom distills many of the key insights that were the foundation for the programming and speaker series at the T.W. Lewis Center for Personal Development. And, more importantly, he shows you the mindset that has been foundational to his success. If we can learn from that mindset, we are surely one step closer to attaining the success we all desire.

In *Solid Ground*, Tom offers a blueprint for living a good and meaningful life. He also dispels many of the myths and mistakes that get in the way of that pursuit—including the kind of fearful, victim-focused mindset that leads people to try to "cancel" those with whom they disagree. That culture is an assault on our freedoms and can cause students to become risk adverse, intolerant, or fearful of standing up for what they believe. Fittingly, he derives those lessons not from textbooks or the latest managerial guide on "best practices." Instead, Tom's insights are drawn from his own life story of trial and error, focus, and tireless work.

The lessons Tom teaches are so valuable precisely because you can't learn them in a classroom. You learn them through experience or with coaches or mentors. *Solid Ground* is a book that gives insight into how to live, not just how to make a living.

Amid all the chatter today about how quickly the world is changing, and how AI will completely upend the way we work, it's easy for young adults to feel anxious about their future. The last thing they need is another lecture about how to capitalize on the latest trends. What *Solid Ground* offers is the opposite of that—a return to the timeless fundamentals of success and happiness and the keys to building a happy and healthy life. And its messages are profound and empowering. No matter what changes lie ahead, we all have it in our power to cultivate the habits and mindset that are essential to success.

—Robert Kiyosaki
Author of *Rich Dad Poor Dad*

ACKNOWLEDGMENTS

I would like to acknowledge and thank the many people who helped to make this book possible. First, my wife Jan, who graciously gave me the space and encouragement needed for a project like *Solid Ground*. I also had a lot of support from some excellent writers and thinkers including Robin Currie, Paul Gallagher, Bill Kauffman, Jeremy Beer, Deborah Huso and Ted Zoller. Each of them helped to make this message more concise, more meaningful and hopefully, more enjoyable to read.

INTRODUCTION

"When you want to help people, you tell them the truth. When you want to help yourself, you tell them what they want to hear."

—Thomas Sowell

I can clearly remember the time when *Solid Ground* was first published in March of 2020. Hardback copies had been sent to the University of Kentucky, and I was excited to give my first book presentation to a large group of honors students on Wednesday afternoon. The next day I was set to go to Nashville with my close friend, Steve Ruschell, to attend the annual Southeastern Conference Basketball Tournament.

That night, after having dinner with some friends in Lexington, I was driving back to my hotel and got a call from UK. They were calling to let me know that, because of the potential spread of the Covid virus, the SEC tournament would be played without fans in the arena! Really? Like everyone, I was stunned and disappointed.

For me, the SEC basketball tournament was a highly anticipated annual trip to Nashville for four days of great college basketball and fun with some of my old college friends. Because of my strong southern roots, and love of SEC sports in general, this event was one of my favorite things. But not this year. The following day, the SEC tournament was completely cancelled, along with the entire 68-team NCAA Men's Basketball Tournament. The Covid-19 pandemic had begun. There was fear in the air, and the world was about to change. It was March 12, 2020.

THE COVID PANDEMIC

America was suddenly in uncharted waters, as we were all trying to navigate the risks and uncertainties of this virus. For most adults over 40, like me, the Covid pandemic was just a prolonged inconvenience. But for many, it imposed regular handwashing, social distancing, masks and even the fear of serious illness or death. Most people suddenly stopped going to the office and tried to work from home—and a new normal began for the entire workforce.

But for elementary school students, high school students, college students and single adults under 30, the Covid-19 pandemic was devastating. The ensuing lockdowns, vaccine mandates, school closures and "remote learning" seriously interrupted these students' normal educational, social and emotional development—leaving many of them alone and isolated. It wasn't long before significant increases in anxiety and depression began, and social media platforms became the primary lifeline for most young adults.

By March of 2023, only three years after Covid-19 began, the National Education Association reported that of all college students in America 44% reported symptoms of depression, 37% said they had experienced anxiety, and 15% said they had considered suicide. Something had clearly changed, but the Covid pandemic was only the beginning.

The years from 2020 through 2024 have proven to be the most disruptive in America since World War II, especially for those born after 1990. What the pandemic made painfully clear was that many of the foundational pillars of our American society had been crumbling. The trends I am about to describe affect us all, but they have affected young people much more.

Historically, students were (and still are, if they're lucky) formed by stable families, church communities, good public schools and universities, and a society that encourages freedom, individuality and risk-taking. For centuries these institutions have provided the *Solid Ground* that was necessary for each generation to develop and thrive.

But today that's no longer the case. The traditional family unit is struggling. Church pews are empty. Public schools and universities are more focused on race and gender than on math and science. And smartphones, social media and texting have significantly reduced face to face conversations and close interpersonal relationships.

These destabilizing trends have been gaining momentum over many years; but the Covid pandemic kicked them into overdrive. Young adults today are struggling to overcome these obstacles in ways that older generations simply did not. And since the foundational pillars of family, church, public education and civic engagement are in trouble, young people are desperately searching to find the *Solid Ground* on which to build a successful and happy life. But before we discuss the path forward, let's take a closer look at some of these trends that are making it harder for many young Americans to achieve their dreams.

THE STRUGGLING FAMILY UNIT

The rise of divorce—and of single-parent households—is the first big part of this story. In the 1960s and 1970s, the divorce rate began to increase, and by 1980, 50% of all marriages were ending in divorce. Over time, the number of children born out of wedlock skyrocketed—from less than 5% of all births in the 1950s to almost 50% of all births in America today.

These trends are not good news for young adults. Studies suggest that children raised by a single parent are much more likely to live in poverty, drop out of school, abuse chemical substances, and even be incarcerated. Plenty of children raised in single-parent homes turn out fine, of course, but the scales are tipped against them in almost every area.

Today, couples are marrying later in life and having fewer children. In 1970, the percentage of people aged 25 to 50 who had never been married was under 10%. By 2018, that number had risen to over 35%. In other words, many Americans are giving up on marriage—and with it, one of the surest paths to attaining a stable and satisfying life. Too often, the lifelong commitment to a stable family is being replaced by casual friendships, relationships of convenience and lives of isolation and loneliness.

THE REDUCTION IN CHURCH ATTENDANCE

Another major predictor of health and happiness is being part of a church or faith community. Many studies have shown that people who are religiously affiliated and attend services at least twice per month are happier, more socially connected, and less lonely than their counterparts. Growing up in Kentucky in the 1960s, I can remember that Christian values were generally held by everyone. And the people that didn't go to church usually felt guilty for not going. But not today.

So, no matter what your personal beliefs are, it is clear that the increasing secularization of America is a worrisome trend. Since 1970, the number of Americans who identify as Christian has dropped from 90% to 63%, and the number of adults who regularly attend religious services has dropped all the way down to 21%. More than half of Americans attend "seldom" or "never". Intellectuals talk about this phenomenon as the "rise of the 'Nones'" because the fastest growing category of religious belief is just that, 'None.' Our founding fathers knew that for America to have freedom, it needed morality. And to have morality, it needed religion.

The Covid pandemic didn't create this decline in religion, but it certainly accelerated the decline in church attendance. Today, 20% of Americans report that they attend religious services less often than they did before the pandemic.

THE DISTURBING DECLINE OF PUBLIC EDUCATION

Along with families and churches, public schools have always been foundational for our society. But anyone looking at the outcomes of our public school system today will see that something is very wrong.

Today in America we spend three-quarters of a trillion dollars per year, yet lag behind most of the other industrialized countries when it comes to the basics like math, science, and reading. This problem has been brewing for decades, but again, Covid put it into overdrive. For most students, "remote learning" was either a source of frustration or a complete disaster. Many stopped attending school entirely and chronic absenteeism in public schools rose from just under 15% in 2019 to almost 30% in 2022. Unfortunately, most of these students will never catch up.

But, the most damaging and destructive trend in public schools and universities is their commitment to "Diversity, Equity, and Inclusion" (DEI). Under this ideology, instead of being judged by their merits, students are sorted into categories based on race, gender or identity preference. And by "equity," they mean promoting the idea of "equal outcomes" over "equal opportunity." This concept of "equity" has replaced "merit" and has led to some states actually eliminating advanced math and A.P. classes.

Over the last few years, DEI has filled buildings with teachers and administrators to promote these ideas. Students quickly learn that this ideology must be embraced and takes priority over hard work and even free speech. Shockingly, 65% of all colleges and universities and 90% of all Fortune 500 companies have implemented some form of DEI.

But, fortunately, this movement is beginning to unravel.

THE NEGATIVE INFLUENCE OF SOCIAL MEDIA

One reason why ideologies like DEI spread so rapidly during the Covid pandemic (in the months following the deaths of George Floyd and Brianna Taylor) is that Americans were consuming more and more media—and often thinking less and less for themselves. As traditional social institutions like families, churches, and local communities weaken, Big Tech and Social Media giants have rushed to fill the gap. Our lives are increasingly spent online, consuming content generated by a few loud voices on big platforms.

What I want to emphasize is that smartphones and social media don't just act as distractions—they teach *distractibility*. They fragment our attention and our ability to focus. And that's a big problem, because success in almost every worthwhile endeavor requires concentration and focus.

Social media also seems to promote a "herd mentality" and forced agreement with popular opinion. Surveys show that most students are afraid to speak up if they think differently out of fear of being "canceled." Social media promises personal expression, even the possibility of being an "influencer," but typically discourages thinking or acting individually. I also think that social media promotes, in part, an increased aversion to risk in many young adults—whether in committing to a relationship, taking a leadership position, or being pro-active in managing their career.

THE ANXIOUS GENERATION

The overall picture is undeniable. Young Americans today are more isolated, less likely to get married and have children, and generally less happy than previous generations. Of those aged 18-25, over 60% report significant anxiety or depression symptoms, and rates of depression and anxiety are ten times higher than pre-pandemic levels.

In *The Anxious Generation*, sociologist Jonathan Haidt makes a powerful argument that social media and smartphones have played a central role in young adults' declining mental and emotional health. In the past ten years, rates of depression, anxiety, self-harm, and suicide have skyrocketed among teenagers and college students. His hypothesis, supported by a lot of evidence, is that these new technologies have wired them for distraction and discontent over concentration and achievement.

Fortunately, parents and educators are now waking up to this threat. I expect more places will follow the lead of Virginia Governor Glenn Youngkin, who recently issued an executive order banning smartphones in all public K-12 schools.

The overall conclusion is that students and young adults today face some real headwinds. So now that we understand the problem, we can begin to address it. And that's what *Solid Ground* is all about.

WHY I WROTE "SOLID GROUND"

I wrote this book as a roadmap to help you find success, purpose, and happiness. But, because so many young adults are getting bad messaging and bad advice on these important concepts, I see them struggling to get started in their lives.

Having interviewed hundreds of high school seniors for college scholarships, and followed them through college and their early careers, I understand the concerns, anxieties, and even fears of the rising generations. Trying to sort through your life choices while constantly being reminded by parents, teachers, and social media to "follow your dreams, do what you love, and find your passion" can be pretty intimidating for a twenty-year-old or even a thirty-year-old.

SOLID GROUND

To be successful in life, I have learned that you have to put first things first—but today's popular culture has it backwards. You can't find your passion until you develop your work ethic. You can't find your purpose until you find your talent. You can't find your happiness until you help others. And you can't find success until you earn it.

I am a builder, not a philosopher, so I have designed this book the way a builder would design a home—from the ground up. In *Solid Ground*, I have presented ten principles from my own personal experiences in sports, education, business, philanthropy and life. These building blocks are timeless, and will help you to stay strong, safe, successful, and even happy, with minimal chaos in your life.

Over the course of my career in homebuilding, I have learned to appreciate the importance of a good foundation—one that is built on *Solid Ground*. When I build a home with a good foundation, it allows the owner to thrive in it for decades with maximal enjoyment and minimal problems.

On the other hand, if I build a home with a bad foundation or on shifting soil, the foundation cracks will eventually extend damage to the framing, drywall, and even the roof. These problems are expensive and often impossible to repair, creating long-term hassles and heartaches for the owner.

So it is with life.

In today's media-driven, anything-goes culture, we seem to be losing sight of *Solid Ground*—the time-tested attributes of personal character, hard work, goal setting, self-awareness, and helping others—that have always been necessary for a successful life. Popular myths are now attempting to redefine everything, and the *Solid Ground* is being replaced with the *shifting sands* of instant gratification, self-absorption, and consumerism.

Among these many popular myths and their corresponding realities are:

MYTH	REALITY
• Following your passion and doing what you love is the key to success and happiness.	• Success is the result of talent, hard work, and persistence. Happiness naturally occurs when you love others, have gratitude, and live a moral life.
• Successful people are just lucky.	• Successful people use their natural talent, start early, work late, set goals, and keep getting better.
• You must choose between success and happiness.	• You can have both, either, or neither, because they are unrelated.
• You can be anything you want.	• You can be anything you are naturally good at…if you earn it.
• Work smarter, not harder.	• Work smarter and harder. It takes both to succeed.
• Thirty is the new twenty.	• Thirty is still thirty, and your twenties are still your defining decade. Successful people don't waste time.
• Balance is the key to life.	• Finding your talent and your purpose is the key to life. Both take time.
• You can build your self-esteem and resilience by taking a class or reading a book.	• Try something hard. Fail. Get back up. Repeat. That's how you build your self-esteem and your resilience.
• Taking risks is too dangerous, and failure is final.	• Taking risks is necessary to get rewards, and failure is an important part of your journey to success.
• Commitment limits your options.	• Commitment eliminates the clutter in your mind and helps you focus on your goals.

SOLID GROUND

Finding success, purpose, and happiness is not simple, and it certainly is not easy. But if you are willing to put in the time and effort to invest in your future, then this book is for you. In these pages, you will find many of the important life lessons I have learned. These lessons have come from my own experience as well as the writings and teachings of many of our best thinkers— from Socrates to contemporary philosophers, and from successful people in all walks of life. From these lessons, I will show you how to build your foundation, reach your potential, and ultimately find life's greatest achievements.

The many ideas and concepts presented here are not all my own. Having read many of the popular books on these subjects, I have also tried to present a compilation or "highlight reel" of the best advice, the best ideas, and the best wisdom I have accumulated. Where possible, I have given credit to the original writers and thinkers.

This book begins with my personal story to demonstrate how your early years and family history can help you understand your roots and how this understanding can lead to purpose and meaning. Then I discuss the building blocks that will give you the stability and support you will need to deal with the challenges and opportunities that lie ahead. Next, we will move to the real-world skills you need to reach your potential. And finally, we will explore life's greatest achievements—success, purpose, meaning, wisdom, and happiness— so that you can better understand and achieve them all.

WHY THIS MESSAGE IS IMPORTANT

My generation had it pretty easy. College tuition was low, and when we graduated, there were a lot of big corporations waiting to hire and train us to do our jobs. There was a clear ladder for us to climb. We also didn't have the distractions of the smartphone or social media. And our cultural values were clear—faith, family, country, and hard work.

Today, navigating the journey to success in career and life is not so obvious. In fact, for many, it is downright scary. What young adults need today, probably more than ever, is a return to the fundamentals of building a good life—one that is full of goodness, success, and even happiness. And it's not really that complicated. This book presents a model for success that has worked for centuries—and it will work today. By getting clear on what really matters in your life and career, your anxiety and fear will melt away, and you can begin your journey to success—on *Solid Ground*.

I wrote this book for you—if, as I suspect, you are a person who wants to find success and happiness, who has dreams and ambitions, and the talent to achieve them, but who, in all the noise and nonsense and clutter of modern life, isn't quite sure how to get where you want to go.

I was once in your shoes. But with a lot of hard work, good decisions, and the confidence to take risks, I made it.

So can you. Here's how…

PART I

MY PERSONAL JOURNEY

Chapter 1

DISCOVERING MY ROOTS

"You can't connect the dots looking forward; you can
only connect them looking backwards."

—Steve Jobs

I n his now famous 2005 graduation speech at Stanford University, Steve
Jobs, cofounder of Apple Inc., did something he had refused to do for
years: share telling details about his personal life. He spoke of being ad-
opted at birth by a good family and of how—to avoid wasting his parents'
working-class income on college—he later dropped out but sat in on classes
that interested him.

One of those classes, Jobs told the graduates, was calligraphy, a subject
that Oregon's Reed College was famous for in those days. Why share this
seemingly trivial detail? Because his skill at calligraphy would, years later,
play a key role in his design of the first Apple computers. That was his
point: the importance of early and diverse experiences.

At the end of his career, Jobs could see with great clarity how his early
life experiences had prepared him to excel at his life's work. These were the
"dots" that connected with each other to create a unique set of experiences
and skills that became clear only in hindsight. The rest is history.

As I reflect on the dots in my life, I can also see that they are connected, just as you will be able to see someday with your life and your dots. Early life experiences, both good and bad, mold you. They help shape your worldview, define your character, and illuminate your values. They also influence your habits, steer you toward your role models, and help you find your talent.

My own "connecting the dots" moment also came on a university campus, in this case at the University of Kentucky (UK), my beloved alma mater. This happened in 2017, at the dedication of the Lewis Honors College, which I had endowed to create a first-class educational opportunity for the best students in my home state.

Mark Twain supposedly once said "the two most important days in your life are the day you were born and the day you find out why." For me, that second date was November 3, 2017.

In my talk, I explained my love of Kentucky, its people, and its flagship university. As a seventh-generation Kentuckian, my affections are deep. I called this love irrational, though it is only irrational in the sense that the emotions of the heart are irrational. But even in a rational way, this love makes perfect sense. It is the love of home and family and of one's roots.

I felt no sadness that weekend, no melancholy, no yearning for lost youth— just a deep satisfaction, a sense of fullness and, yes, pride. This was a payoff of sorts, but in a currency far more valuable than money. In my adult life, I had worked much harder than most. I had a drive to achieve, a drive whose twin engines were my mother, who had always set high expectations and encouraged me; and my father, whose failures—not so much in business, though he had those, but of character—motivated me to restore honor to our family name.

I had finally found, and understood, what I had been looking for all these years. And it wasn't measured in dollars.

Creating the Lewis Honors College was a chance for me to honor my family, my parents, their parents, and the people who came before them. I spoke of the values of hard work and education, of perseverance and returning home. This gift to UK represented the things that had mattered most to me all my life: family, education, personal growth, leadership, achievement, helping others, success, purpose, and yes, even happiness. This event was a culmination of sorts, the climax of a story that began long ago.

But as I thoroughly enjoyed this day and tried to take it all in, I couldn't help but ask myself:

> How did I get here?
> What had I done to put myself in this position?

The answer came quickly: I had built my life on solid ground. This is the story of how that happened.

MY PERSONAL JOURNEY

"You were born an original. Don't end up a copy."

—Unknown

Born into a middle-class military family, I moved around a lot until I was twelve, when my dad retired from the U.S. Navy. Because both of my parents were from Letcher County in eastern Kentucky, we moved to Lexington to be closer to family.

Eastern Kentucky is part of Appalachia, which is known for its coal mining, ruggedness, hillbillies, and poverty. It is a region of the country frequently mocked and ridiculed in popular media. And while there is certainly poverty in eastern Kentucky, there's also pride, and a lot of good people.

Growing up, I spent a lot of time with grandparents, great-grandparents, aunts, cousins, and even second cousins—people who clearly mattered to my parents. I knew they were proud of their ancestors, their relatives, their state, and especially the Appalachian Mountains they called home. But it wasn't until much later in life that I realized the depth of this heritage and really came to appreciate it.

Settlers first came to eastern Kentucky in 1775, when Daniel Boone blazed the Wilderness Road trail through Cumberland Gap. Over the next 100 years, settlers from Pennsylvania, Virginia, and North Carolina came to Kentucky in search of the American dream. Most of those early pioneers were originally from Wales, Scotland, Ireland, and England and were drawn to the rugged country and coal-mining potential of the Appalachian region. But the story of Appalachia, eastern Kentucky, and my ancestors actually started long before Daniel Boone.

BORN FIGHTING

In 2004, American Scots-Irish descendant, Vietnam War hero, and U.S. Senator Jim Webb published a book called *Born Fighting: How the Scots-Irish Shaped America*. I was well aware of my Scots-Irish heritage, but I didn't really understand the history and impact of the group's migration until I read Webb's book. Webb helped me understand a lot about the Appalachian region, my family, and even myself.

During the Civil War, much of the Confederate Army was made up of Scots-Irish descendants who fought with ferocity and bravery. These largely poor whites weren't just fighting to protect slavery; they strongly objected to any outside influence threatening their homeland and were willing to fight to their deaths to protect it. My great-great-grandfather, James "Rebel Jim" Lewis III, was one of these soldiers. To this day, the roots of the American Declaration of Independence, the Constitution, and current-day populist politics can be clearly traced to the Scots-Irish heritage.

Those pioneers carried names like Lewis (Welsh), Jones (Welsh), McIntosh (Scottish), Duff (Scottish), Brown (Braun-German), Smith (English), House (Haus—German), Benge (English), Cooper (English), Collier (English), Reynolds (English), Baker (English), and Boone (English). These people were my ancestors. In fact, Daniel Boone's father, Squire Boone, was one of my sixth great-grandfathers, with Daniel's older brother, Samuel, being my fifth great-grandfather, and Daniel being my fifth great-uncle. It is gratifying to know I can trace my values to my Scots-Irish heritage. It helps explain my nature, which has a strong streak of rugged individualism, something passed down to me by my parents who, naturally, had the biggest impact on my values, my personality, and my whole approach to life.

SOLID GROUND

MY PARENTS

By far, the biggest and best influence on my childhood was my mother, Ruth. Delivered by a midwife in 1920 at Goose Creek, Kentucky, she grew up in a place accessible only by horseback at the time. Her only sister, Faye, was born seventeen months later.

Mom's family loyalty was fierce. "Side with your brother against your cousin, and side with your cousin against a stranger," she would tell me. This was typical of the strong family culture that existed in Appalachia during the Great Depression. I learned very early to value family over non-family and to never give up on a member of your family.

When Mom and Aunt Faye were fourteen and thirteen years old, respectively, their parents sent them to Sayre School, a private boarding school in Lexington, Kentucky. In those days, Sayre was considered a finishing school for young ladies. Mom loved Sayre School and came away with a strong appreciation for proper etiquette, which included exacting table manners, gentlemen not wearing hats in the house, and standing when a lady enters a room. She passed these values on to me.

Mom was very much a child of the Depression—frugal, resourceful, private, conservative, traditional, and optimistic. She also had a gift for wisdom, knew her values, and was very comfortable in her own skin. She was a strong woman, and her influence on me continues to this day.

My father, Thomas G. Lewis (known as T.G.), also grew up in eastern Kentucky, the son of a lawyer and politician. His grandfather, Theophilus Garrard Lewis, was a well-known judge in Kentucky. My fourth great-grand-father, James Theophilus Lewis (born in 1736), had an estimated 11,000 descendants and was a celebrated Revolutionary War veteran from North Carolina.

Daddy's given name was originally Theophilus, which is not a name one wears lightly. As a boy, he took a good deal of ribbing over the name and learned to fight and then box. But by the time he was in the navy, he'd had enough of being Theophilus and legally changed his name to Thomas. I can't say I blame him. Unfortunately for him, he was called to World War II at age twenty-four, spent twenty years in the navy, and was never really able to find his calling.

The oldest of four children, Daddy had twin sisters who were eight years younger and one baby brother who died shortly after birth. I didn't know his parents well, but I think they were pretty tough on him and not very emotional. His father also had a drinking problem and died at age sixty-two. Unlike Mom, Daddy rarely talked about his parents.

Growing up in eastern Kentucky in the 1920s and '30s wasn't easy, but Daddy adapted to this rough environment. With his big hands and natural aggressiveness, he became an excellent boxer, earning his place as a two-time state boxing champion in Golden Gloves competition and later finishing third in his weight class in national competition. A natural athlete, he also lettered in football, basketball, and track at Castle Heights Military Academy in Tennessee, and later at Centre College in Danville, Kentucky.

My father had a strong love for the underdog and the common man. He had a small office at home with a framed quote hanging on the wall: "Mankind's greatest need is better understanding of man. All are victims of circumstance, all are under sentence of death, and all deserve pity." This struck me as a profound and true statement, and this "dot" became an important part of my worldview.

After graduating from Centre College in 1938, Daddy attended one year of law school at Fordham University before joining the navy as a young World War II officer. During the war, Daddy spent four hard years in the Pacific theater on small and large ships. He was shot once in the neck during a Japanese kamikaze attack but recovered after a few months. He had an outstanding war record and advanced quickly to the rank of Lieutenant Commander. But there his career plateaued.

I rarely heard my father speak about his war years. He spent twenty years in the navy, but I'd have to say the last ten were frustrating for him. And when he returned to civilian life, he really struggled. It just seemed like he needed the discipline of the navy to keep him in line.

Daddy loved poetry and often made me memorize poems he read to me. By the age of twelve, I had memorized several epic poems, including his favorite, "Invictus," by English poet William Ernest Henley. I later learned that "Invictus" is a Latin word meaning "not a victim," which was the message I believe my father was giving to me. The entire poem, and especially the last two powerful lines, is ingrained in my head:

"I am the master of my fate."

"I am the captain of my soul."

Daddy was a free spirit, a practical joker, a poet, a writer, and an athlete. He was a man's man—he liked hunting, fishing, poker, and drinking with "the boys." He was not a good businessman or money manager and also not much of a communicator. I believe he tried his best to be a decent husband and father, but it just wasn't natural for him.

MOVING AROUND AND GROWING ROOTS

Mom and Daddy met shortly after the war and married in early 1946. My sister, Karen, was born a year later in Newport, Rhode Island, where Daddy was stationed for officer training. Our family moved in 1948 to Ogden, Utah, where I was born on June 21, 1949.

After living in Ogden for my first two years, we transferred back to Newport, where we lived until I was four. I don't remember much from those days, but Mom often talked about her long walks with my sister and me along the Newport boardwalk, where we strolled by the mansions of some of the initial American robber barons (to use the name hung on them by their critics). Mom was quite impressed with these people and felt these early industrialists were to be admired. There was nothing wrong with making money honestly; in fact, it was worthy of respect.

In 1953, Daddy was reassigned to the Naval Air Station in Jacksonville, Florida, where we lived until I was eight. During our time in Jacksonville, Daddy did two "hardship tours" (Navy-speak for when the family isn't included). One of Daddy's yearlong tours was in Formosa (today's Taiwan).

In 1957, we moved again, this time to the Naval Air Station in Pensacola, Florida. When we first arrived, we lived near the base for a few months as we looked for a home, and Karen and I were enrolled in a local school. We then bought a house in a little town across the bridge from Pensacola called Gulf Breeze, and we changed schools again, making a total of three schools for me in the second grade.

This may sound disruptive, and it was, but as military kids, we learned early how to deal with new places, people, and things. This helped me gain confidence and adapt quickly to any situation—another "dot," as I would later see. This experience also helped me develop resilience. "Grow where you're planted," Mom used to say, and I have often reflected on what sage advice that was.

There is extensive scholarly literature on the subject of military families. Psychologists have found that children who move too often can suffer in later life from an inability to put down roots, make lasting friendships and connections, and participate in local civic affairs. This is encapsulated in the answer many military brats give to the question, "Where are you from?"

"Nowhere."

But in my case, I knew where I was from: Kentucky. Sure, we had bounced around, and I was often the new kid in school, but I had been indoctrinated by the age of twelve with the fact that I had roots. My mom made sure we returned to Kentucky as often as possible. And so to this day, if you ask me where I am from, I'll say Kentucky—even though I've lived in Arizona for a far longer period of time than I ever lived in Kentucky.

FACING ADVERSITY EARLY

The most difficult memory from my Gulf Breeze days was the growing realization that my parents didn't get along well, that Daddy was an alcoholic, and that we didn't have much money. I was around ten when I began noticing this. I would hear my parents argue at night, sometimes loudly, and I would find vodka and whiskey bottles hidden all over the house. One night, I was shocked to overhear them say they didn't have enough money to buy Christmas presents for Karen and me.

As the child of an alcoholic, I learned to always keep my antennae up, because I never really knew how things would be when Daddy came home. When he wasn't drinking, he was fine. But if he had been, he was mean, loud, and threatening. Either way, there was often an uncomfortable tension in the air.

When I was twelve, Mom tried to explain to me what I had already sensed: that Daddy was an alcoholic and that we couldn't count on him. This was tough news for a twelve-year-old boy to hear and perhaps even tougher for a loving mother to share with her son. She was bewildered, frustrated, and had nowhere else to turn. She had grown up in an idyllic family, her parents and their marriage as solid as a rock. She thought all men were like her father. But her husband had not lived up to her expectations.

I'm sure she never considered divorce—that just wasn't done, and besides, she had too much pride.

My reaction at the time was to think about what I could do to help my mom and sister. As the only son, I felt a strong sense of obligation to protect them and was determined to take responsibility for this problem. I had to become, despite my age, an adult. From then on, I didn't want to be dependent on anyone I couldn't count on. But realizing that I had choices to make was a pivotal moment for me. I decided then and there that my life would be different—perhaps the most searing and yet beneficial "dot" I can recall.

MY OLD KENTUCKY HOME

During the years in Gulf Breeze, we took several weeks every summer to drive to Kentucky and visit our maternal grandparents, Buck and Liza Jones (known as "Daddy Buck" and "Granny"), in Neon, Kentucky. Daddy Buck and Granny lived at the top of a big hill overlooking all of Neon (population, circa 1962, about 2,000). I can still remember the steps that led up to their front porch—all sixty-six of them. Daddy Buck (whose real name was John William Jones Jr.) was an engineer for the L&N Railroad for fifty years, from 1908 to 1958. He was a dapper and happy man, loved and respected by all, who had become a pillar of their small community. He was a church deacon, a member of the town council, and owner of the local A&P grocery store. I was always proud when I would hear people in downtown Neon introduce me and say, "This is Tommy Lewis, he's Buck Jones' grandson."

How well I remember spending time in Daddy Buck's chicken house and playing baseball on a gravel road nearby with some local kids. Some days I would just wander off and find an elderly woman sitting on her front porch breaking beans (a Kentucky thing), and I would sit with her and ask questions, keeping her company for hours. I developed a real admiration for these rural folks—the ones some would call "deplorables." These were good and decent people, and I learned to respect them.

My grandmother, Liza Jones, was a kind and loving woman who had lived her entire life in Neon. She wasn't as outgoing as Daddy Buck, but she had a quiet strength. She was the daughter of Wilbur Collier, born in 1865, who was another pillar of the community. Grandpa Collier died in 1961 at the age of ninety-six, so I got to know him pretty well. A widely respected community leader and businessman, Grandpa Collier was a real gentleman. He always wore black trousers with suspenders, a white shirt buttoned at the top with no tie, a black coat, and black felt hat. For some reason, he would usually carry a banana in his coat pocket and offer it to me.

Grandpa Collier and Daddy Buck served as role models for the kind of man I hoped to become. It was easy to see why Mom talked about them both all the time in such glowing terms. They were successful men who were dedicated to their families. They knew how to be both strong and gentle, and they were widely loved and respected. I was lucky to have had them in my life.

RETURNING TO FAMILY ROOTS

In 1961, when I was twelve, Daddy retired from the navy (against Mom's advice), and our family moved to Kentucky. Although Daddy hadn't liked the structure of military life, it kept him in line. Mom insisted on us living in Lexington, a nice university town with good schools, but my father had this idea that he would start a business in eastern Kentucky with his two younger sisters, Joanne and Jennette. They used some land they had inherited from their parents as collateral and took out a loan from the Small Business Administration. It was, in retrospect, a very bad decision.

SOLID GROUND

For the next few years, Mom, Karen, and I lived in Lexington, and Daddy spent most of his time in Hyden, Kentucky. His company, Middlefork Concrete Products, manufactured concrete blocks for use in the coal-mining industry in eastern Kentucky. During high school, I spent most of my summers in Hyden, which was in the heart of Appalachian poverty. For a kid who had grown up in suburbia, this was an eye-popping experience. I stacked concrete blocks during the day (talk about hard work!) and hung out with the local kids in the nearby lumber mill at night and on the weekends. Their names were "Bidge," "Bluepelt," "Meathead," "Beanpole," and "Wooley Booger." These were poor and tough people, but I got to know them well, knew their families, and had dinner with them in their homes.

Working at Middlefork Concrete Products, I could see Daddy wasn't a very good businessman. His office was always a mess, and there was no discipline. He also tended to drink with his employees, which is never a good idea.

It wasn't long before the business was in trouble. Daddy and his sisters filed for bankruptcy in 1966 when I was a junior in high school. Daddy's sisters blamed him for the failure, sued him, and tried to foreclose on our home in Lexington (which Daddy Buck had paid for). Needless to say, this was a major embarrassment and humiliation for our family that Mom took especially hard.

Afterward, Daddy never spoke to his sisters again. He went on to take several different sales jobs, most lasting a year or so, with little success. This also meant I didn't see my cousins for about thirty years. The whole sour experience cured me of ever seriously considering another family business.

My teenage years were often turbulent. Daddy's drinking and domestic arguments frequently forced Mom, Karen, and me to escape to a local motel and "hide out" for a few days until he straightened up. After his business failure, it seemed like he just gave up. In 1972, he was diagnosed with melanoma and spent the last decade of his life fighting it. I was at his bedside holding his hand when he died in 1982 at the age of sixty-six. It was sad, of course, but his dysfunctional behavior over the previous twenty years had become such a problem for our family that we were relieved when he passed away.

It pains me to say that because I always cared for my dad. We usually got along, but it was very different when he was drinking or when my mother and sister were around because of the stress he created. He and my mother were not well-suited for each other, and she placed a lot of pressure on him to be more like her father. I wish he had apologized just once for the problems he caused. But he never did.

His drinking and failures clearly affected me as well. I felt I wasn't as good as the kids who had reliable and successful fathers. We never entertained others at home, and I was uncomfortable in formal social settings. I also learned to avoid arguments. But it did give me something to prove.

However, I came to hold a balanced view of him. He was no angel, but I loved him, understood him, didn't fully blame him, and have always forgiven him. Looking back, his problems caused me to compensate by being overly serious and overly responsible, which can be both a blessing and a curse. I believe his failures gave me the drive to succeed. Restoring my family's dignity, reputation, and wealth became my "why," and it has served me well.

But the primary source of my drive was my mother. As a loving parent and role model, her style was just perfect for me. She had two very strong parenting principles that she always used with me: "Hold your child like you would hold a bird in your hand—gently but firmly" and "The parent is the bow—strong but bending. The child is the arrow. The parent aims the child in the right direction, and lets it go." That's what my mother did with me.

I can't imagine a son having a closer bond with his mother. We were so much alike and always so in tune with each other that we usually knew what the other was thinking. I believe she had two heroes in her life: Daddy Buck and me. She encouraged me, listened to me, showed me the difference between right and wrong, and acted as my moral compass. Whenever she "suggested" I do something, I did it. And, I can't remember ever having an argument with my mom.

I have heard that unconditional love is the greatest, and rarest, of all gifts. With my mother, I benefited from fifty-eight years of unconditional love from her. In many ways, she lived vicariously through me, always reveling in my successes. But mainly she convinced me that I was good, that I was smart, and that I could do anything I set my mind to. At an early age, she gave me a great reputation to live up to, and I could never let her down. Remarkably, I can only remember a few times in my entire life that she ever criticized anything I did. She was my biggest lifelong advocate and my primary source of motivation. Mom passed away in 2008 at the age of eighty-eight, and planning her funeral was the hardest thing I have ever done.

CHOOSING TALENT OVER PASSION

Despite the problems I was having at home as a teenager, some very good things were happening for me at Bryan Station High School in Lexington. I was a good student, but some of my most impactful experiences were with my friends and our football team.

You never forget your best friends in high school. Mine were Al Andrews, Grant Robinson, Bobby Haden, and Vince Sayre, and we all played football. Al was a receiver and linebacker. He loved bad weather, reading, and smoked a pipe at the age of twelve. Grant was the star quarterback and president of the student body. He was the typical "big man on campus" but was humble, kind, and a bit crazy, so he was easy to like. Bobby was the running back (who had recovered from polio as a young boy) and was president of our senior class. Vince was a comedian and a hard-hitting cornerback. As for me, I was a starting cornerback and backup quarterback.

In Kentucky in the 1960s, there were two icons. One was Adolph Rupp, the legendary basketball coach at the University of Kentucky, and the other was A.B. "Happy" Chandler, the two-time governor of Kentucky who sang "My Old Kentucky Home" at most UK home basketball games. Amazingly, at our Bryan Station football banquet in the fall of 1966, Happy Chandler was the master of ceremonies, and Adolph Rupp was the guest speaker. Talk about star power! Al and Grant were the co-captains, and I was the first recipient of the A.B. Chandler award for the highest GPA on the football team. Being a good student and a decent athlete helped me shape a new identity.

What was most remarkable about my high school experience, however, was our football coaching staff. We basically had five head coaches.

15

First there was Dan Haley, the official head coach. Coach Haley was a former UK football player, a leader, a character builder, and a disciplinarian. Then there was Roy Walton, a legendary high school coach in Kentucky who had been fired by a crosstown rival school, Lafayette High School, for getting overly excited at a game and tackling a kid who was running down the sideline for a touchdown against his team. Coach Walton was like Bear Bryant to us, and he was a master motivator. He would literally knock you down with a forearm at practice and then pick you up and hug you. We all loved him.

Our other key assistant coaches were Virgil Chambers, Jake Bell, and Phil Pickett, a former star UK running back. Coaches Haley, Walton, and Bell went on to win multiple Kentucky high school football championships as head coaches at different schools. They were all great role models, coaches, leaders, and character builders. Having them all in one place to coach our team was a unique and life-changing experience for all of us.

After our senior season in the fall of 1966, several of my best friends on the team were planning to play small-college football and extend their dreams. We were all getting some recruiting letters and hoping for scholarship offers. Grant ended up getting a scholarship to nearby Georgetown College and was a four-year starter and star. Al played at Centre College as a receiver, and Bobby also played at Georgetown College. I wondered if I should try to play college football as well. So I looked up Coach Haley one day after school and asked him:

"Coach, do you think I should play college football?"

He gave me that tough, fatherly football-coach look and said, "Lewis, how tall are you?"

"Five foot nine."

"What's your time in the hundred?"

"Under twelve seconds."

"So, Lewis," he said, "what are you going to do if a six foot three receiver with 10.5 speed lines up against you, and you have to cover him all the way to the goal line? What are you going to do?"

Reality sank in. "Coach," I said, "I think I'll just go to UK and major in engineering."

While disappointed, I knew Coach Haley was right. Although football was one of my passions (and still is), I didn't have the talent, size, or speed to succeed in football at the college level. I needed to focus on something where I could compete at a high level…and that was academics. So at age eighteen, I chose to follow my talent over my passion. In hindsight, this was one of the best decisions I ever made.

FOOTBALL PREPARED ME FOR LIFE

What I learned from playing high school football for the Bryan Station Defenders was invaluable. It wasn't about win-loss records or X's and O's. It was about preparing for life. The big reason I still love sports is that it teaches real life lessons. All the drama, thrills, achievements, setbacks, mistakes, disappointments, hard work, adversity, and resilience that can play out in a lifetime unfold over sixty minutes on a football field. And then you win or lose. If you win, you celebrate your victory. If you lose, you focus on getting better. Either way, you move on.

I also learned about competition. When you play sports, it's all about trying to win the game, and someone is always there trying to stop you. You practice and compete against someone else who has also prepared and is competing just as hard. This process builds toughness and resilience. Business, as I later discovered, is sports for grown-ups. You compete with other people in your industry just like you did in high school sports. Sometimes you win and sometimes you lose, but the goal is always to learn and improve.

There is a lot of focus today on teamwork, but if you've never actually been on a real team, the essence of teamwork can be hard to understand. This is what I learned about real teamwork from playing football at Bryan Station High School that eventually helped me run a successful business:

- A strong team requires strong individuals.
- Every teammate is responsible for a different job, and everyone counts on everyone.
- Everyone shares the same goals.

- Everyone has to buy in to the leader's vision.
- Camaraderie and spirit are the heart of a real team.

Toughness was also required … and learned. Our coaches often asked, "Are you hurt, or are you injured?" If you were only hurt (tired, sore, bruised, or exhausted), you kept playing. But if you were medically injured, you were excused to see a trainer or a doctor. Through football, I learned that I could get through adversity.

I also learned that resilience is like a muscle. You build up your resilience by using it. In football, as in life, you get knocked down a lot, and you get back up. You keep doing that over and over. It becomes a habit. That's how you build your capacity for handling adversity and being resilient.

The only way to build resilience is to use your resilience muscles. You can't build that muscle if you're coddled or shielded from adversity. I believe the job of parents and coaches is to make children strong, not necessarily happy. University of Texas star quarterback Colt McCoy's dad once said, "I raised my kids to prepare them for the road, not to prepare the road for them." My mother and my coaches prepared me for the road; and so, in a different way, did my father.

Any football player quickly learns that it takes a lot of discipline and hard work to succeed. For my entire four-year high school experience, we pretty much played or practiced football all year long. Practice, practice, practice. Hard work, hard work, hard work. Then you see yourself getting stronger and better, you feel good about what you have done, and you respect who you have become. In hindsight, this lesson of discipline and hard work was one of the most important "dots" on my path to success.

Coming out of high school, I can remember feeling that I was on the right track. I was very confident that I would be successful at something. I just didn't know what it would be or how long it would take.

Chapter 2

WILDCATS AND TAR HEELS

"When the student is ready, a teacher will appear."
—Chinese proverb

Even before graduating from high school, I was hearing the same two questions that all seniors are asked: "Where are you going to college? And what will you major in?" Everyone was offering advice (one of our high school counselors suggested everyone become a dentist), but as a seventeen-year-old, I didn't have a clue.

Mom—who, like any Depression-era child, valued security—thought I should become an engineer. I remember her cutting out an article from *Time* magazine about how big companies were hiring engineers for "good-paying" jobs. Daddy, on the other hand, who grew up in a family of lawyers and judges and had started law school before dropping out to join the U.S. Navy for World War II, naturally wanted me to become a lawyer. The legal field never appealed to me, however. It was just too theoretical, and I was too much of an individualist. In hindsight, the right path for me was business, which I would get to later.

This was typical family career counseling. The two people who know and love you the most and mean well give you the wrong advice. Why?

Because it's based on *their* values and *their* life experiences, not yours. Yet at that point, I was inclined to listen to them. So coming out of high school, I thought I had two choices: engineering or pre-law.

In the spring of 1967, fate—or, rather, philanthropy—intervened. A prominent local engineer, G. Reynolds Watkins, died in a plane crash, and his family established an engineering scholarship in his honor at the University of Kentucky. The scholarship selection was based on academics, leadership, and athletics. Mom helped me apply—and I got it. This scholarship covered full tuition for all four years at UK, which was $115 per semester.

That's right, a UK education cost a whopping $920 over four years. That small amount is all it took to have such an important impact on my life—certainly a big "dot" for me. This scholarship proved that someone, other than my mother, believed I had the potential for success. I still get tears in my eyes when I think about it. And I suppose that's why, when we were in a position to give scholarships, my wife Jan and I gave over 200 awards with the same selection criteria: academics, leadership, and athletics, adding only financial need.

Soon after receiving the Watkins scholarship, I met with the dean of the UK engineering school to review the different types of engineering to choose my major. My options were electrical, mechanical, civil, or chemical. I knew absolutely nothing about any of these things, but mechanical sounded the best to me, so that became my major. I later found out that M.E. was a four-and-a half-year program, but I wanted to be out in four years, so I needed to cut out all unnecessary electives. I guess I've always been in a hurry, but in some ways, I regret skipping those electives. I would have loved to have taken courses in history and philosophy; although, I've made up for that omission with years of reading and study.

About this time, I read a short book called *As a Man Thinketh*, which was written by a self-taught British philosopher named James Allen. Initially published in 1903, this short volume has become a true classic and has been reprinted many times since. It was the first of many "self-improvement" books I would read, and its message was simple and profound:

"Thoughts lead to actions. Actions lead to habits. Habits lead to character, and character leads to destiny."

The big idea here was that everything begins in the mind: "As a man thinketh in his heart so is he." I was reading this wonderful advice at an ideal time. I was eighteen and just beginning to think seriously about my future, what I hoped to become, and how I would get there.

"Aimlessness is a vice," wrote James Allen, and while I already understood that intuitively, I took the advice to heart. Drive is such an underrated quality. Plenty of self-improvement books talk about passion, but few mention drive. Yet the most successful people are driven.

As Abraham Lincoln once advised an aspiring young lawyer, "Always bear in mind that your own resolution to succeed is more important than any other one thing." I had that resolution; most people don't.

EDUCATION—IN AND OUT OF THE CLASSROOM

Because I lived close to UK in Lexington, I agreed to forgo the extra expense of living in the freshman dorms (assuming we even could have afforded it), so I started college in the fall of 1967 and lived at home my freshman year. I soon found out that at UK there was nothing lower on the social totem pole than a male freshman from Lexington (a "townie") who lived at home and majored in engineering. Every day I drove to campus, parked, walked to class, walked to the library, studied, and then drove home. I met no one. I was a pretty social guy, so it was a bit lonely. But I was also a focused student and needed to prove myself at the college level, so it might have been for the best. My first-semester GPA was 3.8, but I am proud to say, it steadily declined over the next seven semesters.

The beginning of the spring semester brought the fraternity rush, and I discovered a whole new world. Suddenly, I got to meet everyone—all the sharpest guys and girls, all the impressive upperclassmen, and even some of the big men on campus. I had found where the action was, and it was exciting that they were recruiting freshmen like me.

At the end of rush, it came down to Sigma Chi and Sigma Alpha Epsilon. I chose Sigma Chi because my father and grandfather had been Sigma Chis, and I was a bit more impressed with the overall group there anyway.

Soon I was in a pledge class with twelve other guys, including Don Besch from Camp Hill, Pennsylvania; Mark Walker from Hamilton, Ohio; and George Ochs from Louisville, Kentucky. These three freshmen Sigma Chis soon became my roommates, and the college fun began.

Starting in the fall of my sophomore year, I lived in the Sigma Chi fraternity house at 704 Woodland Avenue for three years until I graduated in the spring of 1971. It could not have been more fun, more rewarding, or more educational. After fifty years, these same men are still at the top of my list of best friends.

After I moved into the Sigma Chi house, I quickly learned that studying in the wild and crazy environment of a fraternity house was impossible. So five nights a week I departed after dinner for the Margaret King Library on campus, where I had a regular cubicle from about 7 p.m. to 10 p.m. every night. There I could concentrate on my homework and class preparation. Then I went back to the Sig house and enjoyed all the fun and chaos that forty-eight college boys could dream up.

Although I continued to be a good student and take my classes seriously, I soon realized that mechanical engineering was not my thing. It didn't come naturally, and it was just too technical for me. Yet I never considered changing majors because I was fully committed to graduating in four years—nothing else was an option for me. Although my GPA gradually declined, I ended up graduating with a cumulative GPA of 3.2. Still, I had learned so many good and useful things outside of the classroom that I was satisfied with my overall academic performance.

I never took calligraphy like Steve Jobs had, but I took a course in mechanical drafting that later paid unexpected dividends. I learned how to draw with a pencil, how to read blueprints, and while I never put these skills to use as a mechanical engineer, they became very valuable to me as a homebuilder. I always loved to sit at my table with a quarter-inch ruler and design houses. Over my career, I designed hundreds of them. It was something that came naturally to me, and it all started in drafting class at UK.

SOLID GROUND

OPEN TO EXPERIENCE

During the summer of 1969, after my sophomore year, my good friend Steve Ruschell and I decided we'd been working way too much and that we needed a break. So we did a crazy and memorable thing: we randomly decided to take a bus to Cedar Point, an amusement park in northern Ohio, and eventually wanted to get to New York City to see Wall Street.

So we hitchhiked to New York City, where we checked out Wall Street and stayed at the downtown YMCA. It was a much scarier place than the Village People made it out to be—especially the showers. Quickly running out of money, we hitchhiked to Washington, D.C., and then on to Tampa, Florida, to see some old friends. One of our rides was with a tight-lipped fellow who kept a loaded pistol on the front seat of his pickup. We were relieved when he dropped us off, unharmed.

In the summer of 1970, we did an encore—though this trip was considerably less crazy than the first. My mother, my sister, and I were trying to avoid being around my father, so she suggested spending the summer in Tucson, Arizona. She rented a very nice three-bedroom casita on North Oracle Road, and we had a great time together. I got two different jobs: one picking citrus at a place called Desert Treasures and another as a night bellman at a local hotel on the Tucson Miracle Mile. I also took two electives at the University of Arizona, including one in East Indian culture, which was fascinating to a guy who had only taken engineering classes. My sister, Karen, joined us for this trip, along with my Aunt Faye, so Mom was in heaven.

The trip got even better when Steve decided to come out. He worked with me in the citrus orchard with a group of Mexican laborers, and we had a great time. After one or two weeks, Steve and I decided to drive back to Lexington but wanted to travel through San Francisco, then Salt Lake City, then Denver, Kansas City, St. Louis, and finally on to Lexington.

My friends and I took many exciting road trips during my years at UK, but the best ones were during my last semester in the spring of 1971. College had been so much fun that we wanted our final semester to be the best, so we invented the "College Triple Crown," three major events in epic venues: New Year's Eve in New York City at Times Square, Mardi Gras in New Orleans, and finally the Kentucky Derby in Louisville.

In stark contrast to those experiences, I also managed during this last semester at UK to win the "Most Outstanding Greek Man of the Year" award. This was a pretty big deal, given there were about twenty fraternities on campus, each with close to eighty young men. I've received many awards and recognition for a lot of different things over the years, both in business and philanthropy, but none has meant more to me than this one.

BACK TO BUSINESS

As I was preparing to graduate, I had become interested in the field of construction management, and someone suggested I have lunch with a local businessman named Mr. White, an engineering grad from UK. Mr. White had white hair and owned a construction company called, predictably, White Construction. At that lunch, he gave me two pieces of advice that I never forgot. First, he told me that as I began my business career, I should focus on my net worth, not my salary.

Net worth is your assets minus your liabilities; if you spend all your salary, no matter how high, you've got nothing. As Chris Rock jokes, Dennis Rodman was rich, but Bill Gates was wealthy. Wealthy people don't blow it. Mr. White's second piece of advice was to be as generous as possible, especially with your wife. Both of these ideas resonated with me and became important guiding principles.

Sometime during my senior year, I decided to go to graduate business school to get an MBA. Having always been drawn to the words "construction" and "investment," this decision felt like the right path for me. Business is really all about planning, organizing, motivating, and controlling—which is exactly what I loved doing at UK, and it was all outside the classroom. I knew I wanted to pursue this in grad school, and I wanted to do it quickly.

UK's president, Dr. Otis Singletary, had come to UK from UNC-Greensboro as chancellor. After I got to know him, he suggested that I apply to UNC's graduate business school at Chapel Hill. That advice, and the letter of recommendation he sent to UNC on my behalf, had a lot to do with my decision to go there. Having lived in the South most of my life, Chapel Hill felt like a place where I could both fit in and stand out.

Looking back, when I entered UK in 1967, I wasn't really interested in or ready to learn engineering. I was interested in how to become a leader, how to plan and organize, and how to work with people and projects on a larger scale. Fortunately, I found many good teachers for this. When I got to UNC in the fall of 1971, at age twenty-two, I was ready to buckle down and learn how to become a successful businessman.

CAROLINA ON MY MIND

The University of North Carolina's MBA program was everything I had expected…and more. There were 120 people in my class, and almost all were outstanding. Probably only 20 percent or so had come directly from undergraduate school, so I was among the younger ones at age twenty-two. The average age was about twenty-seven or twenty-eight, with about one-third of the class being married. Our class had 118 men and two women in the fall of 1971.

I was proud to be in the youngest quarter of our class. Today, college counselors advise graduates to go out into the world and get work experience for two or three years before going to business school. Bad advice. Those graduates often just tread water for the two or three years, failing to move the needle or make much progress. Thus, when they finally get their MBA at age twenty-seven or twenty-eight, they're behind those who went straight to business school. That's the competitor in me speaking, I know. But time matters.

One of my strongest memories is sitting in class during the first week with my section of sixty classmates. We sat in a horseshoe-shaped classroom so everyone could see each other's faces. As I looked around, I was trying to decide if I was in the top half or the bottom half, and I wasn't sure on day one. Wanting to excel definitely motivated me, so I set a personal goal of graduating in the top 20 percent of my class, which I accomplished.

But I never did bleed powder blue or pull for Atlantic Coast Conference (ACC) teams. My Southeastern Conference (SEC) roots go way back to my childhood, listening to Auburn coach Shug Jordan on the radio, hearing my mother talk incessantly about the University of Tennessee, and rooting for Kentucky. Those teams had terrific rivalries, but nobody in the SEC hated anyone else. There was just a lot of respect and pride. Not true in the ACC, where everybody still hates everybody, and especially they all hate Duke.

What really impressed me at UNC was the business school faculty. I had never seen people like this before. They were unbelievably smart and could talk about business principles and practices in the most interesting and entertaining fashion. Dr. Gerry Bell was my favorite. He was thirty-five years old, dynamic, and taught organizational behavior—the theory and practice of how people and organizations succeed. He also had just written a book, destined to be a classic, called *The Achievers* (1973) that described six different personality types:

- The Commander
- The Avoider
- The Attacker
- The Pleaser
- The Manipulator
- The Achiever

Dr. Bell's definition of an achiever was someone who could set and achieve goals, get along with people, share ideas, collaborate, and find win/win outcomes. The achiever was the one to emulate, rather than the commander ("My way or the highway"), the avoider ("I think I'll just hide out here in the back room"), or the others. As an engineering major who had taken very few electives, this was my first introduction to psychology, personality types, and self-awareness. I found it both fascinating and useful, and it sparked a lifelong interest in trying to understand myself and others.

With a PhD in psychology, Dr. Bell also provided some profound knowledge about human nature and mental health. One day in class, he described a person with good mental health as someone who had the following characteristics:

- a balanced view of himself, accepting the good and the not so good.

- a balanced view of others, accepting the good and the not so good.

- a balanced view of the world in general, accepting the good and the not so good.

This struck me as a powerful message and explained a lot about life: nothing is perfect. Everything has both positive and negative features, including people. Accept imperfection, and move on. This became an important part of my worldview. You and I are not perfect, nor are we evil. Years later, I put a sign in our office that said: "You don't need to be perfect. You just need to get better."

I also remember a finance professor named Dr. Avery Cohen, who had just written a book called *Financial Decision Making: Theory and Practice* (1972). It was eye-opening to learn that we make almost all decisions under a condition of uncertainty. The key is to use business skills to make smarter decisions—and Dr. Cohen taught us how.

Since the MBA program was on the pass-fail system, the focus was on learning and not testing. I loved going to class and participating and I especially loved the case studies. The case-study method is the heart of a good MBA program. Here's how it worked: The professor gave us a thirty-page summary of a company. Half of it described the people and the business; the other half consisted of data and graphics, charts, and financial information. Our job was to read the case, figure out what the problem was, and create a plan to solve it. Then we discussed and debated it in class.

There were no right or wrong answers. We argued about whether ABC Corporation had a finance problem, a marketing problem, or a people problem. It was usually a combination of many things, but it taught us how to think like executives, look at a complex problem, analyze it, and create a strategy to fix it. We did about three of these case studies a week for two years—an exercise that taught us how to deal with complexity in the real world. This business education left me feeling like I was "dueling with unarmed men" in many of my future business interactions.

Another powerful concept I learned in Chapel Hill was multiple regression. This is a mathematical concept that shows how any outcome can be explained in a formula that weighs all the different causes or variables. Multiple regression helps you focus on the most important variables and not the minor ones, which leads to better decisions.

Soon it was time to interview for a "real" job and begin my career. At that time, in 1973, a dynamic young organization, the Sea Pines Company, was gearing up and planning to go public. It was one of the first large-scale master-planned community development companies that specialized in environmentally sensitive resort properties. I liked Sea Pines—it had impressive young leadership and seemed to offer a lot of early responsibilities and growth. Although it was fairly small, Sea Pines hired forty-four MBAs that year, which was more than IBM. Most were from Harvard, Stanford, and Wharton. They also hired six from my UNC class, and I was among them, along with my good friends Dick Michaux, Marc Bromley, and Bob Shinn. My other good friend, Curt Ensley, was hired by General Electric.

I remember graduating with my MBA on a Friday in May 1973, at the age of twenty-three, and driving to Charlotte, North Carolina, over the weekend to start my new job on Monday. I didn't know what to expect, but one thing was certain: My willingness to learn from a variety of people, places, and experiences had prepared me well—and I couldn't wait to get started.

Chapter 3

BUILDING A CAREER

"There are no elevators to success.
You have to take the stairs."

—Zig Ziglar

Today many young students think the key to success is simple: go to the right college, pick the right major, graduate, get the right job, and you're set. The path will be straightforward, linear, and gradually upward. But it's not. Those students envision their teacher as a wise professor or some willing mentor they meet to teach them the ropes in their chosen field. Nearly any other experience is a diversion and a waste of time. But life experience has shown me that real success occurs differently. It has more to do with being open to learning from a variety of people and places that may seem disconnected or pointless at the time but that will turn out to be key steps in a successful journey. Here's how it worked for me.

JOB NUMBER ONE—SEA PINES

I still remember walking into the main office at River Hills Plantation, outside of Charlotte, North Carolina, on my first day. Sea Pines was primarily a resort developer with projects in Hilton Head, South Carolina; Amelia

Island, Florida; and Puerto Rico; but in May 1973, I had joined the group that focused on "primary home" master-planned community development. It was a prestigious place to start. Because its communities were considered high-end and were growing so fast, Sea Pines had become the darling of the real estate industry.

First there was Harry Frampton, the general manager, then only twenty-nine. Harry had been a salesman at Hilton Head and was a rising star. He was charismatic and personable—and a doer. He also was a master at getting input from everyone and providing a sense of "team." Then there was my boss, J. Roy Martin, the head of construction and development. J. Roy was very experienced, a real Southern gentleman and a stickler for detail. He had an unusual way of communicating that was very effective. If he wanted to tell you something important, good or bad, he would write it on a small note, fold and staple it for privacy, and have his assistant deliver it. Some notes would simply say "Nice job." Others would say, "Please do this over." You pay extra attention to a communication like that.

Champagne in Plastic Glasses

After a few months of training in Charlotte, we all moved to Richmond to begin planning for a 3,000-plus-acre master-planned community that we later named "Brandermill." During this preconstruction phase, I primarily did financial modeling for infrastructure improvements and future commercial real estate projects. For the first year, we met weekly to discuss the vision and strategy of the new community, trying to plan for the next twenty years.

Unfortunately, Sea Pines' business practices weren't nearly as farsighted. Although Richmond didn't have a very large high-income population, the company insisted everything be top of the line. "You don't serve champagne in plastic glasses," they'd say. It sounded good, but the company used this philosophy to justify just about any expense, and it encouraged irrational behavior. Everything was high-end, all marketing and sizzle. But they paid no attention to their expenses.

Back in Richmond, we had begun to focus on land sales, and I was asked to oversee parcel sales to homebuilders. Although I wasn't thrilled to be selling, it introduced me to the world of homebuilders, and I really enjoyed getting to know these people. My new title was director of development unit sales, and I was a one-person department, reporting to Harry Frampton.

Our first customer was Ryan Homes. Ryan, then the third largest homebuilder in America, was new to Richmond. My job was to entice Steve Smith, Ryan's division manager in Richmond, to buy land and build homes at Brandermill. Then there was Buddy Sowders, who had a small homebuilding company called Construction 2000. Buddy was a pure entrepreneur who built small and large homes and also developed commercial projects.

After my second full year in Richmond, Sea Pines' troubles were mounting, and the company began weekly layoffs at all of its resort communities. It was bizarre, even ghostly, to observe the brand new six-story building at Hilton Head—a corporate headquarters built with borrowed money—standing there completely vacant but with a parking lot full of company-owned cars that had been returned by all the laid-off workers. It was as if some lethal virus had wiped out the population while leaving the physical plant unharmed. Something had gone terribly wrong. And a lot of innocent people were paying the price.

Sea Pines wasn't laying off many people in Richmond, but the writing was on the wall. About that time, Steve Smith and I had a meeting, and he offered me a job at Ryan Homes. He wanted to hire me into a training program to become a division manager. Throughout my two-and-a-half years with Sea Pines, I had been learning more about myself, what I was good at, and what I wanted to do. I felt it was time to make a change and try something else.

I had no regrets about my time with Sea Pines. It was a good place to start, and I had learned some important lessons. The high-quality approach appealed to me, but I saw it was driven more by aesthetics than profitability. Management didn't control costs, and their hiring decisions were based on resumés and IQs rather than on experience and ability. Sea Pines also borrowed way too much money, and its managers didn't seem to understand the huge risks they were taking until it was too late. The company ended up filing for bankruptcy just after I left in mid-1975.

JOB NUMBER TWO—RYAN HOMES

When something fails as a result of going to one extreme, people often go to the other. That's what I did. Ryan Homes took a very different approach than Sea Pines did, which suited me fine. Ryan's product was targeted to the mass market. You wouldn't find Ryan in resort communities. If Sea Pines was champagne, Ryan was beer. Ryan was in all the old rust belt cities like Pittsburgh, Cleveland, Rochester, Buffalo, and Dayton.

Ryan was the anti-Sea Pines. Its product was pretty bland, with mostly bi-levels and aluminum siding. This wasn't very exciting—no one was drinking champagne out of anything, plastic or otherwise, but the houses were cost-efficient to build, and Ryan was very profitable with tight cost controls and a proven system. If we can save a dollar on the cost of a door-knob, I was told, and we build 20,000 homes a year, then that's $20,000 more in profit. The guys at Sea Pines would have rolled their eyes at that one.

After driving to Washington, D.C., on a Sunday afternoon to inter-view with Dwight Schar, the regional vice president for Ryan, I was invited to start in a management training program in Richmond. For the next six months, my title was assistant superintendent, but I was basically a laborer. I swept houses, tarred basements, and ran errands. I also worked for several different homebuilding field superintendents with various styles. One of them, Larry, spent an hour showing me the right way to sweep a garage. I never forgot. His attention to detail made a big impression. He had a system for everything, and it made sense.

Working as a laborer might sound like a negative experience, especially for a guy with a degree in mechanical engineering and an MBA, but hon-estly, those six months I spent in the field were probably the most valuable of my career. Rather than being stuck behind a desk, I was out there learn-ing how homebuilding really worked.

I learned that construction is mainly about the "trades," the workers who actually build the houses. Homebuilding is more like hockey than ballet: It's not well-choreographed; it just happens. That means being ready when the trades show up, talking with them to make sure they know what to do, answering their questions, and listening to them. Many homebuilding and real estate executives never get this experience, so they don't really understand or respect the construction process. Thanks to Ryan Homes, I did. After this experience, I could always hold my own with the many construction guys who later worked for me.

Homebuilder Boot Camp

My next stop in the training program was Dayton, Ohio, where I was quickly thrown into the deep end. My initial responsibilities included sales management, purchasing, and customer service—and I knew nothing about any of it.

The Ryan employees in Dayton weren't about to let me forget it either. They all had been doing the same job for about twenty years, and they resented a young "college boy" being given so much responsibility.

Luckily, my boss, a smart and seasoned division president named Don Howells, took me under his wing. Good thing, too, because my coworkers were only too glad to point out my mistakes—which were many!

After a year and a half of being a division coordinator, I moved to the field as construction manager—another job I knew very little about. Now I was responsible for directly managing field construction superintendents. Talk about being intimidated! Fortunately, I was reporting to Hank Motzer, a legendary Ryan employee who had earned everyone's respect, and he had my back. When you saw his station wagon pull into your subdivision, you knew you'd better have your ducks in a row.

The Ryan Homes management system was good at cost control and scheduling, but it completely ignored product quality and customer satisfaction. I saw firsthand the havoc that resulted when a builder delivers a bad house to a customer. It led to disrespected customers, demoralized employees, and it wasted a lot of time and money. I knew there had to be a better way.

From a personal standpoint, those three years in Dayton were miserable. Besides being challenged and criticized by my employees on a daily basis for not being competent in my job, I was single, living by myself, didn't have many friends outside of work, and was suffering the climate of Dayton, the hay fever capital of America. The culture of the division was also tough, as my boss preferred to meet in bars and drink beer while doing business plans on bar napkins.

At least I was learning from my homebuilding boot camp. There were many demanding drill sergeants, a lot of valuable training, and scores of management lessons. Apparently I passed the test because in the fall of 1977, Ryan Homes offered me a position as division manager in Akron, Ohio. At twenty-eight, I would be Ryan's youngest division manager.

I weighed the pros and cons and decided that it was. Mom did, too— she knew it was an important step and encouraged me to go for it. Becoming a Ryan Homes division manager meant something in the housing industry, and it would open future doors. Running a division for Ryan at such a young age would also increase my future market value. We decided I would do it but no stay more than two years. This middle-ground approach seemed like a good way to deal with a difficult decision.

Akron, Ohio

I started cold in Akron—literally—on January 2, 1978, in the middle of a blizzard. The Akron West Division was hot, however. Its young and enthusiastic staff was building and selling about 250 homes per year. But Ryan was an extremely low-risk homebuilder. We optioned all our lots, and my division's maximum quota on unsold spec homes was three. (I later had over 100 at one point in Phoenix!)

I enjoyed working in Akron much more than I had in Dayton. I finally felt like I knew what I was doing, and I was around more people my own age. And because the division manager was such an important position for Ryan, which had about thirty divisions and growing, it provided a lot of management training at corporate headquarters in Pittsburgh. I would go there several times a year for various assessments and personalized feedback.

At one training session, there was an assessment called "The In-Basket Exercise," where instructors gave you a three-inch-high stack of random papers that might be in a division manager's in-basket. There would be contracts, letters, personnel matters. The test was to see if you could connect the dots—like a superintendent resigning and getting a customer complaint from the same neighborhood. You also had to assign relative importance to each matter to decide which are urgent and which can be dealt with later.

SOLID GROUND

The feedback I received was mostly good, but they told me I did a better job managing myself than I did managing others. That was a valuable lesson for a young manager, so I tried to improve.

The Ryan training staff told me I needed to become more persuasive, and they recommended that I take a night class called The Dale Carnegie Sales Course. Grounded in the wisdom of Dale Carnegie, author of the bestselling book *How to Win Friends & Influence People* (1936), the course provided me invaluable lessons about persuasion and getting along with people. Carnegie's timeless twelve rules for winning friends and influencing people include the following:

1. Never criticize, condemn, or complain.
2. Give honest and sincere appreciation.
3. Arouse in others an eager want.
4. Remember people's names, and use them.
5. Talk in terms of other people's interests.
6. Avoid arguments.
7. Begin in a friendly way.
8. Appeal to the nobler motives.
9. Dramatize your ideas.
10. Throw down a challenge.
11. Let the other person save face.
12. Ask questions instead of giving orders.

My Ryan Homes training had given me a grounding in these valuable principles of human nature, and they became the model for how I approached people. These are the kinds of things you just can't learn in the classroom, yet they play a huge role in your future success.

Ryan's culture was about figuring things out and getting them done, not about good intentions, strategies, theories, or twenty-year plans. But paying so much attention to cost and none to product served to undermine the company's goals.

When, years later, the T.W. Lewis Company became the quality high-end homebuilder in Phoenix, it had a lot to do with my experience with Ryan Homes. I would never have been so personally committed to quality and customer satisfaction had I not seen the high price of poor quality that was paid by customers and employees at Ryan Homes.

The Girl of My Dreams

Of course, life isn't all work. In April 1978, an employee of mine talked me into a blind date with her good friend, who was getting her master's in counseling at nearby Kent State University. Her name was Janet Reishtein. Jan and I met at a dinner party, started dating, and really hit it off. We had a lot in common, our family backgrounds were similar, and the relationship grew quickly. After about ten months, we were getting serious.

Then another job offer came from a headhunter in North Carolina. A new homebuilding company in Phoenix named Universal Development Corporation (UDC Homes) was looking for an executive to head its retirement development and homebuilding division. I had been in Akron only fourteen months, but I was ready to leave Ohio and Ryan Homes, so Jan and I took the interview trip together in February 1979.

Phoenix in February is beautiful, in stark contrast to the miserable weather in Akron, so we were favorably impressed. On the flight back to Akron, we talked about getting married and moving to Phoenix together. We planned our wedding for Saturday, April 21, 1979. It was a busy few days that went like this:

Thursday	April 19	Sold two homes and deposited $40,000
Friday	April 20	Last day at Ryan Homes
Saturday	April 21	Jan and I got married
Sunday	April 22	We left on our one-week honeymoon trip to Phoenix
Monday	April 30	Started work at UDC

Our wedding was small and memorable, with our families and all my best UK friends there to share our day with us. We held the reception outside Akron in a beautiful small town called Medina at a restaurant named Great Expectations—a particularly good sign for another new beginning.

SOLID GROUND

JOB NUMBER THREE—UDC HOMES

Jan and I arrived in Phoenix full of excitement and, yes, great expectations. I had already spent one good summer in Tucson, so my enthusiasm for Arizona was high. This was a great adventure for a newly married couple ready for a change. And Phoenix was on the verge of booming. Its population of about one million would quadruple over the coming decades. It was a land of opportunity. In Richmond the question was, "How long have you been here, and who was your grandfather?" In Phoenix, no one cared. The field was wide open.

I was also happy to be starting work for a great new boss. Rich Kraemer, five years my senior, had obtained his undergraduate degree at The College of William and Mary and earned his MBA at Harvard University. Rich was a rising star in the housing industry and a charismatic leader. He had a knack for winning over trades and employees at every level. Jan and I became good friends with Rich and his wife, Carole, and they became our new role models.

My initial position at UDC was vice president and general manager of its 600-acre retirement community in East Mesa called Fountain of the Sun. From its humble beginnings as a broken-down trailer park, Fountain of the Sun had evolved into a lively retirement community with an eighteen-hole golf course, seasonal apartment rentals, a large recreation center, and an active homeowners' association. All these operations reported to me, so I was a big fish in a very small pond.

After about a year at Fountain of the Sun, UDC purchased 1,280 acres on the northwest side of metro Phoenix to create a retirement community that would compete with Del Webb's famous Sun City. Planning and developing this new master-planned retirement community became my primary responsibility. Now my experience with Sea Pines, which others might have written off as a waste of time, became extremely valuable. I knew exactly what to do, and Rich basically left me alone to do it.

Our new retirement community, Westbrook Village, had many different components and introduced me to some new development and business areas, especially in marketing. Del Webb's Sun City, which had opened in 1960, was very well-known, so we thought long and hard about how to help Westbrook Village compete. We decided to emphasize the contrast: Sun City was a city, Westbrook Village was a village; they had lots of circular streets, ours were meandering; they had concrete, we had grass. It was a good plan, and it worked.

All my previous experience came into play here. I had learned about land planning and development at Sea Pines and about designing and building homes at Ryan, so I felt very comfortable and ready to manage all of this. Rich gave me a pretty free rein, as he was busy starting a "family home" operation in Phoenix and in San Diego. This was a very exciting project for me. I knew my skill set was rapidly expanding, so I was really enjoying my job. Except for one thing.

Metropolitan Phoenix covers a lot of space. It was about seventy-five miles from Fountain of the Sun in East Mesa to Westbrook Village in northwest Peoria—the same distance that separated Lexington and Cincinnati. Jan and I had used our $40,000 in savings as a down payment for a home in Tempe, which was about twenty miles from Fountain of the Sun and sixty miles from Westbrook Village. In short, I was driving a lot of long distances every day.

And our family was growing. Our first son, Tommy, was born in January 1981, followed by our second son, John, in April 1983. Jan had become a full-time mom, so she was worn out by the time I was getting home, which— thanks to me working late and then getting stuck in rush-hour traffic—could be quite late.

Not surprisingly, I could feel the enthusiasm for my job sinking fast, and I started thinking about another career move. The excitement of Westbrook Village had worn off, and my job had turned into a grind. I also couldn't see much of a future for me at UDC. A very small circle of key people there were reaping the benefits of our success—and I wasn't one of them. I'd been there five years, and it was time for another change. But even though I was ready to make another career move, I couldn't resign from UDC without a new position lined up. That's a hard and fast rule. The best time to get a job is when you have a job because you have more leverage.

I didn't see any better alternatives. But then another good thing happened. I was sitting in my office at Fountain of the Sun one afternoon in early 1984, when I got a call from Dick Michaux, my classmate and good friend from UNC. Dick had also worked at Sea Pines and Ryan Homes and had just accepted a position with Trammell Crow Residential out of Dallas as the partner in the Washington, D.C., area. Trammell Crow, then the largest real estate developer in America, was looking for a partner in Phoenix to start a new division. Dick asked if I was interested. You can imagine my answer. I've always been grateful to Dick and, by extension, to UNC, for giving me this opportunity.

I ended up interviewing with longtime Trammell Crow partners Tom Teague and John Carmichael out of Dallas and Houston, respectively, and they offered me the job.

My annual salary at UDC had been $80,000, but the culture at Trammell Crow was that partners make their money on successful deals with *no salary.* They called this compensation plan "eat what you kill." I ended up agreeing to a 10 percent partnership interest with a $40,000 salary in year one, with my salary going to zero in year two. That's right: zero. With a home mortgage and a growing family, I took a big leap of faith. Some people would call this a big risk, but—reminded of the laid-off Boeing executive I had worked with in Las Vegas—I was more worried about the risk of being dependent on someone other than myself. This wasn't a rash or reckless decision. It was a calculated risk that I had thought long and hard about, and I was confident that I could make it work.

JOB NUMBER FOUR—TRAMMELL CROW

In the real estate industry, as in most industries, it is difficult to make the transition from employee to owner. You need a lot of capital, for one thing, and you need to convince yourself that you're ready and able to take the risk. Crossing this divide can be as difficult as crossing the Grand Canyon, and Trammell Crow became my bridge.

My experience with Sea Pines, Ryan Homes, and UDC had taught me a lot about managing sales, construction, customer service, product design, and people. But I had no real experience in finance, deal-structuring, and risk management. Any business has three key elements: sales and marketing, finance and accounting, and operations (construction management or manufacturing). Almost everyone has a strong suit, and mine was in operations. Although I had learned a bit about finance at UNC, I really had no practical experience in this area. Luckily, Trammell Crow was the perfect place to learn.

I have to credit the Trammell Crow family with creating a perfect culture. They only hired partners who were well-educated, entrepreneurial, and driven to succeed. They gave those partners tons of freedom to build new apartments and to do whatever residential projects they wanted. But they also made it perfectly clear they expected results.

Two or three years later, Trammell Crow Residential decided to combine its various residential divisions under one umbrella. Ron Terwilliger from Atlanta was selected over Tom Teague as the managing partner. Although my loyalty was with Tom, I also had great respect for Ron, whom I knew from Sea Pines and who had been Harry Frampton's boss when I was in Richmond. Ron, another Harvard MBA, was an exceptional leader and executive.

Not long after this reorganization, Trammell Crow promoted me to regional partner, overseeing projects in Arizona, New Mexico, Colorado, Nevada, and Utah. At age thirty-seven, my income potential had increased significantly, and I was in a position to really start growing my net worth, something I had been working on since my conversation with Mr. White when I graduated from the University of Kentucky.

As a regional partner, I also became a member of the National Trammell Crow Residential Board. It consisted of Trammell Crow himself, Ron, and three national partners: Dick Michaux, Leonard Wood (another UNC friend), and Bob Speicher. We met about every six months to discuss overall strategy and results. This was an impressive group of people, and I felt fortunate to be sitting at the same table.

A real highlight for me was getting to know Trammell personally. When our Phoenix division made its first profit distribution to the Crow family for their share, I enclosed a short note to thank Trammell for offering me this opportunity. I soon received a handwritten reply that simply said, "Tom, thank you for the distribution, and for your spirit! Trammell."

That generous attitude was contagious. People said Trammell Crow succeeded because others wanted him to. Trammell was a real estate legend and an even nicer man. I never once heard anyone say anything about him that wasn't complimentary. Perhaps he sometimes trusted people too much, but everyone loved and respected Trammell and his wife, Margaret.

During my time at Trammell Crow Residential (1984 to 1991), I developed over twenty different new apartment communities and about 5,000 apartment units. These communities were mostly in Phoenix with several in Albuquerque, two in El Paso, one in Santa Fe, and one in Denver. But with the single-family housing market down in Phoenix in the mid-1980s—and my background in homebuilding from Ryan Homes and UDC—I decided to start a homebuilding division under Trammell Crow Residential (TCR) in Phoenix. I hired another Ryan Homes alumnus, Warren Hunter, to lead this operation, and we bought our first project in late 1986.

Then, in 1988, Ron fired the TCR partner in Denver who also had started a homebuilding business, and he asked me to get involved. So, in early 1988, my responsibilities included an apartment operation based in Phoenix under a sharp young partner named Bruce Ward; Trammell Crow Homes in Phoenix under Warren Hunter; and the homebuilding business in Denver, which was managed by a bright, inexperienced young lady named Joy Gilbert.

Homebuilders and Airplanes

There is a saying in the homebuilding world that "when homebuilders get on airplanes, bad things happen." I was about to find out how true this was. Without an experienced manager in Denver, I made the trip about every other week for two days at a time to get this operation going, and it wasn't easy. Apartments are relatively easy to develop from a distance, but homebuilding is local. I didn't know the people, the trades, or the competition, and the market was terrible. TCR had committed about $1.2 million in cash to get this division started, and we were just trying to stay alive until the market got better.

When we ran out of cash, I sent out a capital call to the other partners, but they didn't want to invest another dime, so they told me to wind down the operation. When I explained this plan to our lender, a German bank, they panicked and froze our funding, so we couldn't make payroll. Then most of our employees quit, and our trades walked off the job with about forty homes under construction.

Unfortunately, things weren't much better back in Phoenix. Our homebuilding business wasn't doing very well, cash flow was unpredictable, and our financial statements were in poor shape and usually late…which is never good.

The real estate market across the nation was struggling around that time (1990), so I wasn't surprised when Ron called me to explain that TCR had decided to eliminate all non-apartment businesses, including home-building. He gave me a choice: I could either close it down and stay with TCR as the regional partner or take over the Trammell Crow Homes business myself and go it alone. He asked me to think about it and come to Atlanta in a few days to talk with him in person.

I knew Trammell Crow Company was coming under a lot of pressure nationally in its commercial business, and lenders were beginning to deny the company any further credit. In Phoenix, our local and national lenders began asking tough questions about the strength of our loan guarantees. Our top construction lender in Phoenix was Valley National Bank, whose real estate department was headed by David Blackford. He and I were friends and were having lunch at the Phoenix Country Club about this time, and he told me he couldn't make any more loans to any Trammell Crow entity—but he said that he could make loans to me. Hmmm.

The writing was on the wall. After seven years with TCR, I was finally ready to start my own company. Ron, TCR, and my top lender had presented me with the opportunity. This was a classic case of preparation meeting opportunity, and I knew I had to seize the moment. It was a big risk, but so was staying put. I knew I was ready to make this commitment and realize the dream I had in Chapel Hill when I was twenty-three.

TCR and I soon worked out a simple transition agreement and set things in motion for my exit from the apartment business and its exit from the Trammell Crow Homes business. It was the summer of 1991. I was forty-two years old and had worked for four great companies and at least six outstanding bosses over eighteen years. I was as ready as I would ever be.

Chapter 4

GROWING A COMPANY

"Go out on a limb. That's where the fruit is."

—Unknown

My experience at Trammell Crow Residential left me sure about two things: It took a lot of money to start a homebuilding business and a lot to wind one down. Thanks to the transition agreement that I worked out with my TCR partners, we avoided these problems. The TCR partnership, which included me, wouldn't face any wind-down costs, and my new company—with six active communities, a backlog of homes under construction, an office, and about thirty existing employees—would avoid the startup costs. It was a win-win arrangement. And since I had started this business from scratch, it felt good to "buy out" my partners in this way and move on. We were hopeful we would recoup a million dollars from the wind-down, and we ended up making twice that.

From Trammell Crow, I had learned much about the benefits of partnerships. But I had also discovered that they can break under stress when things go wrong or when partners disagree. The very word "partnership" in

Japanese, in fact, is often translated as "same bed, different dreams." Now *I* had all the risks, all the upside, and just *one* dream. But with all my chips on the table, there was no room for error.

Learning from my previous failure was a big advantage. Reflecting on the experience I'd had with TCR in Denver, I could see that it had basically been a half-hearted plan, poorly executed. We had made the most fundamental mistakes:

- We didn't know the market.
- We weren't committed.
- We were undermanaged.
- We were underfunded.
- We didn't have a clear plan.

This disaster was starting to look like a blessing in disguise, because it taught me several things *not* to do. It also made it clear that I needed help in several key areas—strategic planning, accounting, and marketing.

HOW ARE YOU GOING TO COMPETE TO WIN?

There's an old piece of cowboy wisdom that says "sometimes you need more horse, and sometimes you need more harness." When you start a company, you need more horse—that is, sales. Then comes the harness: the systems that ensure profits, quality, and customer satisfaction. When I decided to run my own business, I didn't have much of a horse and no harness at all.

My first call was to Martin Freedland, an organizational consultant from Atlanta who was deeply involved in the for-sale housing industry. Martin, who had helped me structure things at TCR, introduced me to an annual homebuilder conference in Vail, Colorado, called The Presidential Seminar. Led by longtime housing guru Lee Evans, the seminar offered sessions on management principles, including profitability, cost control, managing people, and market positioning. It routinely attracted all the best private homebuilders and housing consultants in the business.

That meant it was an excellent place to network, as Jan and I discovered when we attended our first Presidential Seminar in January 1992. On a van ride from the airport to the seminar, we met Dave Stone, a very well-known housing expert in the area of sales and marketing. We hit it off right away and arranged for him to visit Phoenix to help with our sales and marketing plans.

Dave was a wonderful and enthusiastic person with knowledge, experience, great judgment, and rock-solid instincts. Author of the books *New Home Sales* (1982) and *New Home Marketing* (1989), he was a real pro who proved instrumental in helping me name and brand my new enterprise. He showed us where to place our models in a new community, how to create a sales phasing plan to build momentum, and how to manage salespeople, which can be especially tricky.

Dave visited us at least twice a year for the next ten years, and his philosophy of sales and marketing became ingrained in our culture. Dave believed there was a perfect home for every buyer. The job of the salesperson was to help the buyer find the perfect fit. He also introduced me to another Presidential Seminar consultant named Steve Dudley, whom I hired to help us create our business strategy.

In our first meeting, Steve asked me one of the best questions I had ever heard: "How are you going to compete to win?" Framing anything as a competition, of course, brings out your best. And figuring out the answer helped us come up with a plan to differentiate ourselves in the crowded Phoenix housing market.

The need to stand out was obvious. In 1992, Phoenix was easily one of the top three largest housing markets in America, and there were nearly thirty large public homebuilders knocking heads with each other at the low end of the market. It was easy to get lost in the crowd, and as I had learned at Westbrook Village, I needed to be different. But how?

I had worked for two public homebuilders, and both had measured their success by the *quantity* of homes they built, not the *quality*. I found this approach common in the industry. Whenever I asked a homebuilder to describe his company, he would say something like, "We build 100 homes a year." Or 1,000, or 10,000—and that's it. None of them, incredibly, ever mentioned anything else, especially the word quality! I was beginning to see my opportunity to stand out in a crowded market.

So when Steve Dudley showed me this simple two-by-two matrix and asked, "What box do you want to be in?" I knew the answer:

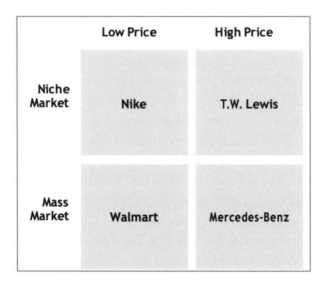

	Low Price	High Price
Niche Market	Nike	T.W. Lewis
Mass Market	Walmart	Mercedes-Benz

Competing to Win

Almost all the big Phoenix-area homebuilders were in the Low price/ Mass market "Walmart" box, because that's where they could get the most volume. To compete and win, I needed to be in the High price/Niche market box. I needed to focus on quality, not quantity.

Fortunately, this strategy aligned with my strengths, my values, my history, and my experience in the industry. It wasn't just a way to be different in the marketplace. It was not a gimmick. It was real. From my personal experience, I was genuinely committed to the ideas of product quality and customer satisfaction. And deciding who we wanted to be also helped clarify who we *didn't* want to be.

But, I wasn't born to be a homebuilder. You don't come out of the womb with that stamped in your DNA. I had to learn it, and it had to be authentic, not a marketing scheme. I really cared about taking the hassle out of home buying for people, and it came through. No one else in Phoenix had anything close to that outlook, and we turned it into profits. I understood if I could deliver on the promise of quality, I could command more sales and higher profits.

We were now ready to come up with a name, a branding position, and a vision statement:

> **Name:** T. W. Lewis Company
>
> **Brand Position:** Homes for Particular People
>
> **Vision:** T.W. Lewis Company will become the best homebuilding organization in America as measured by product quality, customer satisfaction, and profitability.

This vision was inspiring to me and to all our employees. It incorporated the key takeaways from my four previous jobs and combined them into one vision that would express my dream, my values, and my personal journey.

We then rolled out a marketing campaign that featured my name, our brand position, and my face on a billboard:

T.W. Lewis Billboard

In order to stand out, we needed a bold strategy, and this was it. In Phoenix, no one had ever seen a homebuilder's face on a billboard, especially with a promise like that, and it got people's attention. The thought was that anyone willing to put his name and face on a billboard must be trustworthy.

After all, I'm looking you right in the eye. We did some limited television advertising but found billboards more effective. We ran these same billboards from 1996 through 2008, and built a well-known brand and reputation for quality in the Phoenix market.

I got a kick out of this marketing campaign because it really worked. Even now, almost 20 years after the last billboard came down, people in Phoenix still often recognize me, but mostly they remember our quality.

We also created a little plastic card for our employees to carry, one that would be clear about who we were, who we weren't, how we operated, and what we stood for. I was convinced this strategy would help make us both different *and* better.

	OUR PURPOSE	OUR MISSION	FOUR PILLARS OF EXCELLENCE
T.W. LEWIS QUALITY SINCE 1991 HOMES FOR PARTICULAR PEOPLE	T.W. Lewis Company exists in order to contribute to the quality of life for our customers, associates, trades, and community.	T.W. Lewis Company will become the best homebuilding organization in America, as measured by product quality, customer satisfaction, and profitability.	1. Style & Design—unique and sophisticated 2. Construction Quality—unsurpassed 3. Better Buying Experience—from sale through service 4. Proactive Service—on time, with a smile

T.W. LEWIS COMPANY IS DIFFERENT THAN ITS COMPETITORS BECAUSE:	FIVE CUSTOMER PHILOSOPHIES	CORE VALUES	
We care more about quality than quantity. We are customer friendly. We are guided by specific values.	1. We are ladies and gentlemen serving ladies and gentlemen. 2. If it's wrong, we'll fix it. If it's right, we'll explain it. If it's gray, we'll talk about it. 3. The Particular home-owner isn't always right—but usually is. 4. All problems are treated individually 5. We believe in compromise as a way to resolve issues in a win-win manner.	**Honesty** Telling the truth, not cheating or stealing, being honest in all interactions. **Hard Work** Going the extra mile, voluntarily, to get the job done right with a sense of urgency. **Reliability** Making good on your commitments. Following up as expected. Being on time. Being dependable.	**Integrity** Showing consistent uprightness of character in our words. Saying what you believe, and doing what you say. **Achievement** Setting goals, striving to improve, getting results. **Compassion** Understanding other people's point of view. Showing empathy, caring, and kindness for others.

T.W. Lewis: Purpose, Mission, Difference, Values

I had once heard that any CEO who couldn't describe how his company was different in twenty-five words or less was running a company that was in trouble, and I couldn't afford to let that happen to me. The message on this card became the identity and culture of our organization. We knew our purpose, our differences, and our values. And we would stay out of trouble.

Over the next several years we focused on our systems for accounting, profit margins, construction quality and customer satisfaction. According to many, these systems became the best in the Phoenix housing market and among the best in America.

Trammell Crow once said, "You don't do right because it's good for business. You do right because it is right. But it does help your business." We ended up getting plenty of word-of-mouth referrals, but we never had to ask for them. Sometimes why you do things is just as important as what you do.

From 1992 through 1998, we had been adding three to four new communities each year, for a consistent annual volume of about 280 homes, with twenty to twenty-five closings per month. We also entered our first America's Best Builder award competition in 1998. This meant completing an exhaustive application that evaluated each applicant on every facet of its business, including sales and marketing, construction management, people management, trade partnerships, finance and accounting, and continuous improvement. In the category of homebuilders under 500 homes per year, we won the award as America's Best Builder in 1998.

After eight years of continuous feedback and improvement in customer satisfaction, we finally reached the 98 percent-plus level, which Woodland, O'Brien & Associates called "bulletproof." This meant our reputation for quality was beyond question. According to Woodland, O'Brien & Associates, the national guru of customer satisfaction in the homebuilding business, we had become one of the top two or three homebuilders in the country for consistently achieving high customer-satisfaction ratings. And we were making a lot of "particular people" very happy.

Obviously, we were thrilled to receive this kind of recognition and validation. A lot of hard-working and dedicated people had bought into our vision, and this was the result. This was a high point for my company and for me. We had been in business for only eight years, and we had accomplished our goal, but this milestone achievement came with some things I didn't expect.

REACHING THE TOP OF THE MOUNTAIN

Months away from my fiftieth birthday, I began to reflect on my career, my life, its purpose, and what my future should be. I had been driven to succeed and had worked sixty-hour weeks for twenty-six years to achieve it. I had a wonderful wife, three sons of whom I was very proud, and more money than I ever thought I'd have.

But I also had a somewhat empty feeling—and considerably less enthusiasm for the homebuilding business. I felt like a mountain climber who had spent his life moving from one level to the next and then, when he's finally at the summit, finds himself disappointed with the view. Was this all there was? Was this achievement worth the price I had paid? What had I missed? Should I sell my company? If so, what would I do next?

I was clearly at a personal crossroads. I needed some new inspiration and purpose to guide the next chapter of my life. I needed a new mountain to climb—one that would challenge and motivate me. And one that would provide a deeper sense of meaning.

After giving serious thought to selling my company, I opted for a middle course: I would retain ownership and control but hire a new president and chief operating officer (COO) to run the daily operations. This seemed like another good compromise: I wouldn't have to sell my company, but I'd have more free time to pursue new things.

Our new COO, Kevin Egan, was an excellent manager of people and processes, and he was much better at delegating than I was. We shared the same values and attitudes, so I was fortunate to have him—especially at the start of what turned out to be a major market upswing. It wasn't easy releasing control, and as the saying goes, the only thing harder than running your own company is not running your own company.

Over the next few years, the Phoenix housing market mirrored the market in other parts of the country, going from good to hot to white-hot. Phoenix's new housing volume had increased from about 30,000 annual new home starts in 1999 to over 60,000 in 2005. Our annual home sales had grown from about 240 per year to as high as 400 in 2004, and our average sales price went from $325,000 in 1999 to $730,000 in 2006.

This major increase in volume meant that our organization also changed dramatically. We'd had fifty to seventy-five employees in the 1990s, but by 2006, we had 140 employees and had added a new corporate office building, a full-service design center, an IT department, a human resources department, and a marketing and public relations director. We even had an in-house architectural department and had created our own separate mortgage business. In other words, the management demands had grown significantly.

Our business model had also expanded to include a land acquisition and development department under the leadership of Pat Adler, a smart and hardworking executive with a degree in civil engineering and an MBA. We then began to acquire larger parcels of land (200 to 400 acres) to develop our own multi-neighborhood master-planned communities. Soon we had increased our land debt to over $50 million with another $50 million in construction debt.

From 2002 through 2006, we had made our ambitious vision a reality. Our banker told us we had the highest profit margins in Phoenix.

And in product quality and customer satisfaction, no one else was even close. If there was a better homebuilding company in America during those years, I don't know who it was.

By the end of 2006, our annual home closings were about 320, and annual revenue peaked at $236 million. Due to this market surge, the profit margins were way up, too! It was almost too good to be true, and we thought it would last forever. Until it didn't.

PLAYING DEFENSE

By early 2007, it was clear that things had changed. The market had gotten so hot in 2005 and 2006 that we had started a lottery system to select and limit the number of our homebuyers. Most builders, however, weren't this prudent. Instead, they were taking huge numbers of sales with little earnest money, then falling behind in their ability to get houses built. Because we remained committed to quality over quantity, we stuck with our program and limited our sales to four per community per month, while other builders were taking advantage of the market and selling ten to twenty homes a month in each neighborhood.

The lottery lines got shorter and shorter, and then stopped. Prices had increased so much, fueled by easy home mortgage credit and speculators entering the market, that buyers became nervous and started canceling in large numbers. By the end of 2007, our net sales had fallen to about 150, and due to cancellations, we had over 100 unsold spec homes. Yikes!

With nearly $100 million in outstanding debt, we had a problem. Malcolm Gladwell was right. In his book *Outliers: The Story of Success* (2008), he demonstrates that success almost always results from hard work, talent, and good fortune. We had put in the hard work, and we had some talent, but we also had the obvious good fortune of a runaway housing market in a boomtown. And now that boom was over.

My days in grad school at UNC had taught me there were two ways to approach business decisions. One was to maximize profits, and the other was to minimize losses. This was the time to minimize losses.

Then I got an idea. Some potential buyers had asked if we would rent a house to them. We came up with a plan to create a new company to buy twenty of our oldest spec homes. We would put down 50 percent of the value with our own equity and borrow the other 50 percent from small banks so we could pay down our $50 million construction loan to J.P. Morgan.

Our longtime chief financial officer, Gina Self, did a wonderful job of finding small local lenders to do this, so we were able to initially take out twenty spec homes. Then we added swimming pools, landscaping, and window coverings to convert them into rentals. We paid our salespeople to rent them, and our construction and service staff handled the maintenance and customer service. They quickly rented, so we bought another twenty, and then another twenty, and another, and another until we had accumulated a rental portfolio of 120 homes by the end of 2009.

Because we had retained all of our profits over the last few years, we had a strong balance sheet and were able to pay off our J.P. Morgan debt entirely, shifting half of it to a group of six smaller lenders. This was a much safer position for us than having all our loans with one big bank that could cut our funding at any time. (Thank you, German bank, for teaching me such a valuable lesson.)

By the end of 2009, home prices in Phoenix had dropped by 50 percent, our sales and starts were down to 100 homes per year, and we had gone from 140 employees to forty. That was the bad news. The good news was that we had no debt on our homebuilding business and were free of the severe operating restrictions that banks were putting on other homebuilding borrowers. We had put ourselves in a position to manage the recession in a way we could control— one where we could minimize our losses.

We still owned about 250 lots, but land and lot values had dropped about 50 percent since their peak value. The best way for us to liquidate this inventory was to build more spec homes, finish them, and sell them for the best price we could get. Our goal was to sell just 100 homes a year and keep the doors open. We continued this program through 2010 and 2011. Between the spec building and the rental homes, we were able to keep our forty employees busy. And because we had kept our best people, morale was actually pretty good. I believe our people appreciated the fact that we had handled the market drop so much better than other homebuilders had. We were certainly taking losses, both in land and homes sales, but by the end of 2012, our cumulative losses were less than 20 percent of cumulative profits since 2000. We had been able to keep the other 80 percent, while most builders had lost 50 percent or more of their gains over this same period.

I look back with pride on how we reacted when the music stopped in 2007. Those were some of the best business decisions I have ever made. And even as a veteran homebuilder, I learned a new lesson, and I haven't borrowed a nickel since.

MOVING ON

Despite my satisfaction in how we handled the recession, that six-year period from 2007 through 2012 was hard. It seemed like every day there was just more bad news. I was doing my best to keep myself and my employees motivated and positive, but this grind was taking its toll. I may not have been ready to sell the business in 1999, but I was definitely ready now.

By early 2011, I made a short list of three homebuilders to whom I would consider selling my company. Although it wasn't worth nearly as much as it would have been in 2005, we had a very good organization and a great reputation for quality and customer service. My main priority was to provide a good place to work for my remaining employees, many of whom had been with me ten to twenty years.

At the top of my list of potential buyers was David Weekley Homes, a large private builder out of Houston, Texas. I had met David a few times at national homebuilder events but knew his president, John Johnson, much better from my time with Trammell Crow in Denver. John and David

Weekley's regional president, Jim Rado, had visited me several times in Phoenix, and we had remained in touch.

In May 2011, I called John and asked if David Weekley Homes would be interested in buying our homebuilding business. They had been waiting for the right opportunity to re-enter the Phoenix market, so they were interested. We scheduled a visit within the next two weeks for John and David to come out and see our operation. They liked what they saw, and I felt comfortable with them. They were clearly people of integrity who cared about their employees and customers, and I thought it was a good fit.

We agreed to make a deal. I came up with a proposal for them to buy the operation—much like the deal I had made with Trammell Crow in 1991, except this time I was the seller. I flew to Houston on June 21, 2011 (my sixty-second birthday), to meet with David and finalize our agreement. They had a sixty-day due diligence period, and we closed the sale in September 2011.

I finally began to see some very welcome white space on my calendar and was looking forward to life with less stress. It had been forty years since I graduated from UK and twenty years since I had started this business, so I was more than ready for a change. For all those years, I had been driven by a desire for success, wealth, and the admiration of others. These motivators had served me well and had proven to be a big competitive advantage. But by the end of 2011, I was ready to move beyond them—and find a higher calling.

Chapter 5

FINDING A HIGHER CALLING

"If at first you succeed, try something harder."

—John C. Maxwell

What happens when you reach the top of your personal mountain? We're often so focused on climbing higher and overcoming obstacles that we hardly give this a second thought. "Success is its own reward," the saying goes. But take it from me: Success can present its own problems.

That's not to say I didn't feel proud of what I had done. During my forty years in real estate development and homebuilding, I had accomplished a lot. My style was to be "all in"—fully committed to my family, my job, and my personal success. And because I had earned the self-confidence to continue to raise the bar for myself, that success felt pretty good.

Dealing with the hard work, the risks, and the stress came naturally to me. Problem solving was rooted in my independent Scots-Irish DNA as well as in my hardwired personality and values. My childhood adversity, along with my business experiences, had prepared me well. And I was lucky to have had this combination of drivers.

But the problem with success and with being a highly motivated achiever is that you can never get enough. "Man's needs are insatiable," my dad told me at an early age, and he was right. The more you get, the more you want. And there will always be other people who have more than you.

I had encountered this fact of life before, of course, whenever I reached one of my goals. Over the years, I had learned that the key to dealing with always wanting more was to avoid giving free rein to my appetites—to be satisfied with having just enough and then move on to try to find real meaning and purpose. But now that I was at a professional peak, I wondered: Move on to what?

RETIRE OR RE-FIRE?

Most of my friends seemed to have their own answer to the question of "what next?" Some wanted to keep making business deals and "die with their boots on." Others played golf four times a week, read books, and traveled. And some just wanted to spend time with their grandchildren. These choices all sounded good to me, but none of them really seemed like the best use of my time and talents.

Retirement, I knew, wasn't for me. Spending more time with family and friends sounded appealing, but I wanted to stay active and engaged and do something meaningful while helping others. I hoped to explore some uncharted waters, continue to achieve difficult things, but also find time to let my heart sing. From a financial point of view, I no longer needed to work, but I still needed to be useful. It was going to take some time to figure this out.

Fortunately, I had already laid some groundwork. Before I decided to sell my homebuilding business, I had learned about a career-change strategy called double-tracking. The idea is that instead of staying on one track and then suddenly jumping to another, you go down two tracks at the same time for a while—testing the waters, to mix metaphors, on the new track before completely letting go of the old one.

The five-year partnership transition I had worked out with David Weekley Homes gave me this opportunity. I could still be involved in homebuilding and other real estate investments, but I could spend most of my time with our charitable foundation, exploring ways that Jan and I could make a difference.

In 2001, Jan and I had established the T.W. Lewis Foundation to give back to our community. We did this because we had excess wealth, and we felt a responsibility to help less fortunate people in our community. We began with college scholarships for high-potential students in financial need. We later expanded our giving to include nonprofit organizations that helped children and families in need, and it grew from there.

My overall approach to philanthropy resembled my approach to running a company. To maximize our chances of success, we developed a clear vision and strategy that would make us unique and authentic—just as I had when creating T.W. Lewis Company and its "Homes for Particular People" slogan. We figured out where we wanted to focus, and then we looked for the best nonprofit organizations in each area. The goal was to forge a long-term partnership with organizations whose interests aligned with ours and where our support would lead to greater impact for them and more joy and satisfaction for us.

HALFTIME

While gearing up for our commitment to philanthropy, I spent some time talking with a man who knew the topic well: David Weekley. A generous, smart, and very respected man, David had been devoting half his time and income to philanthropy for well over twenty years, and doing it with a business-like, results-oriented approach that resonated with me.

David introduced me to Al Mueller and his company, Excellence In Giving. Al's company specialized in working with private donors to help them get more impact and satisfaction with their giving. His wide experience with others would prove invaluable.

In our first conversation, Al suggested I attend a three-day program in Dallas called Halftime. Created by Bob Buford, a very successful business-man who became the well-known author of *Halftime: Moving from Success to Significance* (2015), this Christian focused program was exactly what I was seeking.

Although I had been raised as a Christian, baptized at age ten in Gulf Breeze, Florida, attended church as a child, and always been a believer, I had drifted away from my faith over the past thirty years. And I was disappointed in myself. By age fifty, I knew I really wanted to become a much stronger Christian, but I didn't know exactly how or where to begin. Halftime, which provided instruction and personal coaching to help people transition from career success to discovering God's calling for them, was my opportunity to find out.

At this program, I heard from other successful people who were searching for their calling, trying to learn God's plan for their lives. I talked with many who had already found this calling, and they seemed full of commitment and peace. They had found their purpose by combining their talents, their experiences, and their hearts to discover how they could best serve God's Kingdom. Each one had, literally, a mission from God. And like all worthwhile missions, it began with a vision, passed through many struggles, and then became a journey.

I had been pondering these questions even before my trip to Dallas, so it didn't take long to see I had some work to do. I was already working with many different nonprofits involved in foster care, homelessness, domestic violence, character development, and college scholarships and had learned a lot about each of these organizations and what they needed to make a bigger impact. I clearly had a heart for mothers and children in crisis and for helping young people become the best they could be. And I wanted to help other people become successful; not necessarily businesspeople or leaders, but people who could build their lives on solid ground. Thus rooted, they could reach their God-given potential. Everyone deserves that.

THE UNEXPECTED CALL

In June 2013, a few weeks after attending the Halftime program in Dallas, Jan and I were celebrating my sixty-fourth birthday at our home in Flagstaff, where we often escaped the summer heat in Phoenix. Being a fair-skinned guy who lived in the desert and whose father had died from melanoma at sixty-six, I had recently had a routine dermatology check at the Mayo Clinic in Scottsdale, and they had seen a spot that looked suspicious. The doctor told me not to worry, but he wanted to do a biopsy. I had had many biopsies in the past and had never had a major problem, so I wasn't too worried about this one either.

That Friday night, as Jan and I were getting ready for dinner, I got the phone call that no one wants to get. Dr. Robert Orford was calling to let me know that the biopsy indicated a melanoma tumor on my right tricep. He would email me a copy of the biopsy report, but said I should schedule an appointment on Monday to come in to discuss surgery.

Suddenly, everything changed, and life stood still. In an instant, all those things that had seemed so important now seemed irrelevant. Having watched my dad battle melanoma for ten years with radiation, chemotherapy, hospitals, and waiting, I couldn't believe this was now happening to me. As soon as I hung up, I remember having two simultaneous thoughts. One, that my life would never be the same. And two, that somehow this was the wake-up call I needed and would lead to something good.

For the next week, I got busy. I scrambled to get more information on melanoma: the best doctors, the best hospitals, and the best advice. I also posted a request for advice on a website for melanoma victims. After a few days, it seemed clear my best options were the Mayo Clinic in Scottsdale or M.D. Anderson in Houston, one of the largest and best cancer centers in the world. As I was trying to figure out who to see at M.D. Anderson, I got a phone call that had to be divinely inspired. The voice at the other end introduced himself as Mel Klein, a melanoma survivor, who also happened to be chairman of the board of M.D. Anderson. He had gotten my name from a mutual friend and was calling to invite me to come to Houston to get treated. He said I only needed to make one decision—where to go— and then it was out of my hands. He said M.D. Anderson was the best melanoma center in the world; he recommended Dr. Merrick Ross as my surgeon; and he told me they would work me in as soon as I could come to Houston. This intervention was a miracle for me and an answer to my prayers. But it was just the beginning.

SOLID GROUND

We scheduled surgery for mid-July, so I had about two weeks to just think and worry. Unless you have had cancer, this feeling is impossible to understand. I remember my father telling me that once you have the "Big C," you are never the same. It's particularly hard for someone with a take-charge attitude to deal with the feeling of not being in control. You wake up in the morning, and it takes a nanosecond to remember what your problem is. You try to be optimistic, but when you're all alone with your thoughts and fears, you can't help but think the worst.

All my life, I had heard ministers and church members talk about having a personal relationship with Jesus Christ, but I had never really understood or felt this before, but now I did. As I took time to pray to Him in my time of need, it felt like He was with me—that I had a new and compassionate friend. And the realization that the outcome of this ordeal was all in His hands was very comforting.

Finally, it was time for the surgery, which lasted five hours. With melanoma, a surgeon focuses on removing as much flesh as possible to prevent the cancer from spreading. Melanoma cells multiply fast, and if they get into your lymph system or bloodstream, they quickly spread to the rest of your body, and you are in big trouble—stage 4 cancer, which is what happened to my father. If the cancer spreads, the treatment options are chemotherapy, immunotherapy, or some sort of clinical trial. This can go on for years, consuming your thoughts and your time—and it rarely ends well.

Besides removing the area around the melanoma, surgeons take biopsies of the surrounding lymph nodes to determine whether the melanoma has spread. If it had, I would be on the stage 4 path. If not, I would be cancer-free. It would take another ten days to find out. And that gave me plenty of time for more worry. But it also enabled me to reflect on the meaning and purpose of my life. I didn't want it to be over, and I didn't want it to be wasted. If I could be graced with more time, I promised God I would put it to good use.

Thankfully, the call from M.D. Anderson brought good news. The seven lymph node biopsies were all clear. After more than a month of waiting, worrying, hoping, and praying, my prayers had been answered. I had gotten my life back, and I was out of the woods—at least for now.

T.W. LEWIS

THE GREATEST STORY EVER TOLD

"People plan. God laughs."

—Christian saying

And then it hit me. Through my childhood adversity and exposure to the poverty of eastern Kentucky, I had gained empathy and respect for people in need. I also had been blessed with a good brain, a strong work ethic, a solid education, a loving family, and the ambition and drive to succeed. These blessings had all led me to a place where I had excess wealth and a lot of time. Now I knew what to do with both—or at least where to start.

I had endured the toughest thirty days of my life, but I had a lot more clarity about my purpose. More significantly, I felt like I was embarking on an important mission—one that was not about me. Indeed, it was much larger than me. It was God's mission for me to use my talents, resources, and energy for the good of His world, His Kingdom, and His glory. That's the way He works. It had been God's plan for me all along, and now He was revealing it to me. His plan for me became my purpose. It had taken a long time to play out, but looking back, the dots all connected. As Clemson football coach Dabo Swinney once said, "Finding God's calling for your life is the perfect 'why.'" It was for me.

In the wake of the Halftime program and then my melanoma experience, my priorities changed. I was sure I wanted to take my Christian faith to a new level. But first I needed to know a lot more about the Bible, its characters, its stories, and its messages.

Through my Halftime connection, I found a men's Bible study group that was discussing a book simply called *The Story* (2011) by Max Lucado and Randy Frazee. This book covered the Old and New Testaments and was written in an easy-to-read novel format, presenting all the major biblical stories in chronological order. This overview was perfect for me because it explained and connected all the main stories, leaders, and prophets of the Bible from Abraham, Isaac, Jacob, Joseph, David, and Solomon to Jesus.

After reading *The Story*, I was ready to take a deeper dive into the New Testament, which covers the earthly life of Jesus Christ. For six months,

I carefully read and studied each of the twenty-seven books of the New Testament from Matthew, Mark, Luke, and John all the way through Revelations. And what an incredible story this is.

The New Testament is much more than a religious textbook. It's packed with timeless wisdom that has been used in almost every self-help or motivational book ever written. The Bible resonates with the human spirit and is nothing short of the greatest story ever told. That is why it is the bestselling book of all time.

My overwhelming takeaway from reading the New Testament was that it was real—and pure. Jesus' life and ministry radiated love, kindness, grace, humility, forgiveness, compassion, generosity, loyalty, strength, and goodness. There was no self-righteousness, no superiority, no hypocrisy, no mean-spiritedness, and no dogma. In fact, Jesus opposed the strict rules of the temple leaders, making Him a threat to the establishment and ultimately leading to His crucifixion. Jesus, who exemplified the loving and patient nature of God Himself, is the best role model we could ever have.

Among the many powerful messages in the Bible is that we are all sinners and that we will someday individually face God, and He alone will judge us. This truth not only helps each individual become better, but it also helps create a stronger and better society.

Another strong Christian principle I have come to appreciate is grace, or undeserved forgiveness. The Lord's Prayer says, "Forgive us our trespasses, as we forgive those who trespass against us." The Bible teaches us that forgiving others is a noble thing, and it allows us to heal our deepest wounds with others. I was impressed by the sheer goodness of the New Testament. Now, every morning when I wake up, I say a prayer of gratitude. The world has not gotten happier over the past few years, but I have.

CHRISTIAN PHILANTHROPY

Anyone who's serious about philanthropy knows it's harder to give money away effectively than it is to earn it. I've worked with dozens of individual nonprofit organizations, and most have great missions and people who really care. Their common shortcomings are usually organizational problems, poor accountability for results, or a lack of financial stability. That's where we usually tried to help the nonprofits improve. But as my faith deepened, so did my understanding of Christian philanthropy.

With Christian philanthropy, we begin with the premise that my wealth is not really my wealth at all. It's God's wealth because He gave me the tools, the opportunities, and the good fortune to earn it. Because my wealth is His, my role is that of steward, not owner. It's my duty to see that His money is well spent to support His Kingdom here on earth. This is a serious responsibility, but it is also a joyous one. And this responsibility has given me renewed energy, enthusiasm, and purpose.

Our giving is not limited to money (wealth), but also includes giving our time (work), our talents (wisdom), and our advocacy (witness). These four W's—wealth, work, wisdom, and witness—form the foundation of Christian philanthropy.

The Bible is full of warnings about the love of money, noting it is the root of all evil. Instead of hoarding it, the Bible encourages us to give freely to help the poor and the needy, just as Jesus did. As Christians, we are called to follow His lead, realizing "it is better to give than to receive." With this attitude, our giving has greater impact. It's more joyous and more meaningful because we're not doing this for ourselves but for a much higher purpose.

MOVING BEYOND

When I speak about "moving beyond," I am talking about moving beyond the tangible things that drove me for over forty years—success, wealth, and admiration. And I am not alone. These are often the underlying motivators for most successful people I have known, and they help explain why some people succeed more than others.

These drivers are part of the DNA of high achievers, and they include equal parts of self-confidence and "something to prove." These might seem like opposites, but they are, in fact, complementary. This trait combination generates a strong desire to achieve, but it also has a tendency to push the achievers to keep accomplishing even more. At some point, it's time to move beyond these motives.

Success and wealth are pretty obvious motivators, but let me explain what I mean by admiration. When I turned fifty, I read a book by Alice Miller called *The Drama of the Gifted Child* (1997). Miller describes what can happen when a talented child is raised with excessive praise. Everyone likes to get some praise and positive feedback, but a person can get hooked on admiration if too much of his or her self-worth depends on the admiration of others.

This was clearly part of my childhood and the close relationship I had with my mother. Mom praised me constantly, and even though I enjoyed it, I realized that a good share of it was undeserved. There was an upside to her doing this: She gave me a great reputation to live up to, and that made me feel I could never let her down. But I became accustomed to admiration, and it became addictive. It's a good feeling, but it demands you do more.

It took me awhile to realize the desire for admiration had a grip on me that I needed to release. To move on to purpose, meaning, and happiness, I had to let go of success, wealth, and admiration. And to do this, I needed some help.

FINDING MY PURPOSE

In April 2017, I got another unexpected phone call. After the melanoma surgery in 2013, I had been taking proactive PET/CT scans every six months as an early warning protocol to make sure the melanoma didn't return. For three years after my initial surgery, all my semi-annual checkups were good, but that April, the scan showed some tumor activity in my liver and lungs. Biopsies showed I had melanoma again. This time, it was the dreaded stage 4 phase. This is exactly what had happened with my dad, and now it had happened to me.

M.D. Anderson in Houston gave me a new immunotherapy drug called Keytruda that had only been out for a few years. Keytruda changes a person's natural immune system so it can identify and destroy melanoma cells. Because we had caught the melanoma early through the proactive PET/CT scan, the tumors were still very small. For the next nine months, at three-week intervals, Jan and I traveled to Houston for the immunotherapy infusions while Keytruda did its magic.

The moment of truth is when they do the first scan at the three-month mark. Is it shrinking or growing? If the melanoma tumors are shrinking, it's a sign the drug is working. If they're growing…well, Houston, we have a problem. Then they have to try another drug, and it's a race against the clock.

Those were a difficult three months—the toughest I've ever had to endure. But my newly deepened relationship with Christ was a strong source of comfort and peace. I'm not a superstitious person, but because my birthday is June 21, the number 621 means something to me. During the long wait to see if the Keytruda was working, I kept seeing the number 621. On digital clocks, computer screens, street signs, everywhere. Someone was aware of what I was going through, and the message was "You're going to be okay. You're going to have more birthdays."

After three months, the tumors had shrunk by 50 percent, and after six months, only 2 percent remained. After nine months, the melanoma was completely gone, and at twenty-four months, it was still gone. By the grace of God, my lease on life had been extended, and I took this as a clear message that God had spared me for a reason.

Although I wouldn't wish this experience on anyone, I'm kind of grateful it happened. It reminded me there is always a silver lining in the darkest of clouds. Taking a full year off to fight and overcome this life-threatening disease gave me plenty of time for serious reflection. And it allowed me to gain complete clarity on my purpose.

The "dots" were now all connected, and the purpose of my journey was clear. It was simply to find my talents and give them away.

PART II

THE FOUNDATION OF SUCCESS

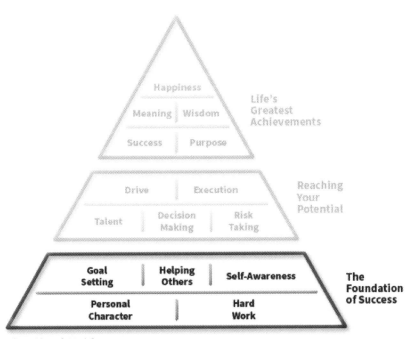

The Achiever's Model

Chapter 6

THE POWER OF
PERSONAL CHARACTER

"We cannot rise above the limitations
of our character."

—John C. Maxwell

I n part I of this book, I told my personal story so you can understand
how I have learned these principles. Part II, "The Foundation of Success," outlines five fundamental requirements for long-term success in
your life and your career. These qualities will set the stage for a happy and
successful personal life and put you in a position to win in your career. Part
III, "Reaching Your Potential," explores five more success drivers that have
largely been overlooked in popular writings. These are the real and important skills that will help you reach higher levels of success and, ultimately,
approach your potential and reach life's greatest achievements. The model
looks like this:

The Achiever's Model

In the following chapters I will define, clarify, and discuss the meaning of each of these characteristics so that you can better understand their importance and incorporate them into your life.

SOLID GROUND—A FOUNDATION FOR WINNING

"Before we can start winning we have to stop losing."

—Brian Kelly

As a longtime homebuilding executive who has built over 5,000 high-end homes over a twenty-year period, I've learned a thing or two about the importance of a solid foundation.

A good home, one that has few problems and allows you to enjoy living there, must be built on a solid foundation. The same is true of a good life; it must be built on a solid foundation of personal character.

Personal character is the combination of all your attributes and characteristics. Being a person of strong personal character is essential to having a good life. Without strong personal character, any success will be short-lived. No one is perfect, but getting clear on what these traits are, and what they mean, will help you improve your personal character and avoid making a life-altering mistake.

I learned this early from observing my dad. He was very personable; I can almost guarantee that you'd have liked him if you'd known him. But he had a serious flaw—his drinking. He also lacked discipline, self-control, and was irresponsible with his money. And his irresponsibility put our family in a tough position. I'd contrast my father with my grandfather, Daddy Buck, who had solid personal habits and made good decisions. These habits resulted in a happy family life and personal success. He was a man who had strong personal character, and that made all the difference in his life.

THE CHINESE BAMBOO TREE

You could say that building your life and your career is like growing a Chinese bamboo tree. Like any plant, the Chinese bamboo tree needs sunshine, water, and nutrients to grow. You plant it, water it, nurture it, and for the first four years, you see no visible growth. You begin to wonder if you're wasting your time. But then in the fifth year, it suddenly grows very quickly and dramatically, up to 100 feet in only six weeks.

How does this happen? For the first four years it grows its root structure, unseen by those of us aboveground. It establishes a system of deep roots that anchors and nourishes it for years to come—roots that make its future growth possible. Without this root structure, the tree would simply collapse, just like a home built on bad soil, a marriage built on infidelity, or a business built on a lack of integrity. A big part of your own root structure is your personal character, and it takes a lot of patience to create that root structure.

WHAT IS THE GOOD LIFE?

"What we do to others, we do to ourselves."

—Bryant McGill

The study of personal character, virtue, and ethics is as old as mankind itself. Prior to 400 BC, Socrates asked, "How should we live?" His answer: "Live the good life!" But what is the good life? Contrary to what many people assume, it has nothing to do with material gain: having a large bank account, living in a big house, driving a fancy car. No, for Socrates, the good life is a life of virtue. He further advocated the pursuit of knowledge and wisdom ahead of personal interests as the best path to happiness.

The history of man's quest to define personal character, or virtue, goes back over 2,000 years to Plato, a student of Socrates and a teacher of Aristotle. Plato was the first to really examine the virtues, or habits of excellence, that a person needs to be truly happy. Though he discussed all these virtues, Plato paid special attention to the four that later became known as the cardinal virtues.

"Cardinal," a name given to the virtues by Christian scholars much later, comes from the Latin word for hinge, because all the other virtues hinge, or depend, on these four primary ones:

- Justice. Giving each person what he or she deserves.
- Prudence. Having wisdom and good judgment.

- Courage. Facing both physical and moral adversity.
- Temperance. Having all things in moderation and exercising self-control.

What we call personal character today is what Socrates and Plato meant by virtue. A person of strong character is one who holds these virtues—he or she is the kind of person with whom we want to associate and the kind of person we want to be.

Throughout human history, great thinkers have agreed: Good habits lead to a good life, which makes happiness and fulfillment possible. This is as true today as it ever was, maybe more.

WHAT IS PERSONAL CHARACTER?

"Ability may get you to the top, but it takes character to keep you there."

—John Wooden

Because personal character involves the combination of all your different attributes and traits, it can be hard to understand. Plus, the list of possible attributes and traits is very long, further clouding what actually makes up personal character.

Two recent books provide insight, however. In *The Road to Character* (2015), David Brooks separates character into two categories: "eulogy traits" and "performance traits." The former traits are the ones that make you a good person. They're the things people appreciate about you and might say at your funeral—that you were kind, generous, and humble. The performance traits, by contrast, are the ones that help you perform and be productive. Examples include hard-working, disciplined, and resilient. Performance traits make you successful but not necessarily a good person.

In *The Only Way to Win* (2012), performance psychologist Jim Loehr, whose clients have included the likes of tennis great Monica Seles and Olympic gold-medal speed skater Dan Jansen, also divides character into two categories, which he calls "moral character" and "performance character." He provides an excellent list of specific traits under each category and creates a scorecard for evaluation. Loehr then points out that moral character and performance character are independent of each other, so it is possible to be very strong in some areas but weak in others.

I spend a lot of time working with nonprofit organizations whose mission is to build character. In a world that is losing its connection to religious faith, the cultivation of character grows harder and ever more important. And most organizations trying to teach it don't really know how to define it.

Several years ago, I was working with a small nonprofit whose mission included "building character in youth," so I began supporting their efforts to expand. Its leaders soon produced an article about their personal character development program, and it started with their definition: "Personal character means doing what you feel in your heart is right." In other words, everyone gets to define his personal character around his own feelings.

I have learned there are actually two schools of thought regarding personal character, and they are very different from each other:

1. Personal character is based on individual feelings, commonly called emotivism.

2. Personal character is based on clear and objective standards for moral behavior.

As you will see, I am clearly in the second camp and believe the feelings-based approach is way too vague and self-focused to forge real character in anyone. It can also be harmful, as it implies "if I feel it, it must be right," which is not always the case.

With emotivism, all moral judgments are simply based on personal feelings or emotions. Another strong focus of the emotivism model is the concept of well-being, which includes personal health, proper diet, exercise, and safety, without any specific standards of moral behavior, with the possible exceptions of kindness and mindfulness. These are all good things, but they are only a very small part of real personal character.

SOLID GROUND

In *The Tragedy of Moral Education in America* (2014), author James Davison Hunter writes, "Implicit in the word 'character' is a story. It is a story about living for a purpose that is greater than the self...The story that is implicit within the word 'character' is one that is shared, it is never just for the isolated individual." But Hunter continues, American culture today has ceased to believe in that story. Instead, "American culture is being defined by more of an absence, and in that absence, we provide children with no moral horizons beyond the self and its well-being." The "emotive" approach exhibits this problem. It forgets about our duties to others, and emphasizes only the well-being of the self.

I'm a guy who likes clear definitions, and you really can't teach something like character until you have a good understanding of what it actually means. That's why when I started my company we came up with the six specific core values mentioned earlier: honesty, integrity, hard work, reliability, compassion, and achievement, along with their definitions. Our employees understood exactly what we expected of them, and it made a big difference.

Based on my personal experiences and what I believe it takes to succeed in your life and your career, I have divided personal character traits into two categories that, with a nod to Jim Loehr, I'll call moral and performance.

MORAL CHARACTER TRAITS

"In matters of style, flow like a river. In matters of principle, stand like a rock."

—Thomas Jefferson

Success in your life is not always about you, but about your relationships with others. In alphabetical order, these are some of the most important moral character traits, along with my definitions:

- Compassion. Understanding and appreciating other people's points of view. Showing empathy, caring, and kindness for others.

- Courage. The golden mean between fear and recklessness, it enables you to take action for what you believe. It comes in many forms, including physical, emotional, and moral.

- Decency. Treating everyone with respect and kindness, and being considerate of others. There are only two kinds of people: the decent and the indecent.

- Faith. Believing in something you know to be true, even though you are not able to prove it. It requires trust in something much bigger than yourself.

- Generosity. Giving freely to others, which can include donating your time, your attention, or your money. It is an active way to show others you care.

- Honesty. Consistently telling the truth. Not lying, cheating, or stealing.

- Humility. Having a modest opinion of your own importance. Putting the needs of others ahead of your own with a heart of service. Acknowledging the wisdom and goodness of others.

- Integrity. Showing consistency in your thoughts, words, and actions. Saying what you believe and doing what you say.

- Kindness. Being respectful, friendly, and considerate of others. Going out of your way to help others. Being unselfish.

- Loyalty. Standing fast and showing your allegiance to the people, groups, and ideas that matter most to you. Like many other traits, it is best demonstrated under stress.

- Respect. Showing others how much you value them and giving them their due. To earn it, you first have to give it to others.

- Trustworthiness. Earning the confidence of others through integrity, strength, or ability. It comes in two forms: You can trust someone's intentions, or you can trust his or her competency. As Dennis Prager says, "Trust is the natural result of being trustworthy."

PERFORMANCE CHARACTER TRAITS

"If you have integrity, nothing else matters. If you don't have integrity, nothing else matters.

—Alan Simpson

In contrast to success in your personal life, success in your career is about you and your relationship with yourself. These are some of the most important performance character traits, along with my definitions:

- Achievement. Using effort, ability, and courage to set goals, get results, and continually improve. It marks the progressive realization of a worthy ideal.

- Assertiveness. Saying what you mean and what you want clearly, but in a manner that demonstrates kindness and respect for others.

- Competence. Possessing the skill and capacity to perform a key task correctly the first time.

- Discipline. Having the self-control to establish and follow a regimen that leads to accomplishment of a worthy goal.

- Hard work. Going the extra mile, voluntarily, to get the job done right. Working with a sense of urgency.

- Judgment. Displaying the ability to understand a complex issue and see the most important factors at a given place and time. Knowing what to do when.

- Perseverance. Possessing the will and stamina to continue pursuing a goal despite obstacles, resistance, or discouragement.

- Reliability. Making good on your commitments. Following up as expected. Being dependable.

- Resilience. Having the ability to recover quickly and fully from setbacks, adversity, and hardships. Having the strength to endure.

- Responsibility. Taking ownership of a problem, a project, or a person. Holding yourself accountable and not making excuses.

- Responsiveness. Responding in a timely and considerate manner to the needs of yourself and others.

- Self-control. Having the ability to control your emotions, words, and actions in a manner that shows respect for others.

WHY DOES PERSONAL CHARACTER MATTER?

"Thoughts lead to actions. Actions lead to habits. Habits lead to character. Character leads to destiny."

—James Allen

While it can take decades to earn a great reputation, you can lose it in an instant with a serious breach of character. And while having consistent good character will lead to many positive outcomes, it is also most valuable in preventing bad outcomes. Without strong personal character, any success we achieve will be short-lived or forgotten.

In matters of overall personal character, no one is perfect, but we can all be better. Consider Benjamin Franklin. Though a hugely successful man by any measure, widely acclaimed even within his own lifetime, this legendary Founding Father never stopped trying to strengthen his own personal character.

In one of the most famous passages of his autobiography, Franklin describes how, when he was just twenty years old, he created his own list of thirteen virtues (temperance, silence, order, resolution, frugality, industry, sincerity, justice, moderation, cleanliness, tranquility, chastity, and humility) and set up a system to develop and reinforce them. Why? Because, as he freely admitted, he, too, often slid into patterns of unproductive and even harmful behavior, and this wise man knew the best way to counteract that tendency was to sharpen his character.

The more time you spend thinking about your personal character, the more conscious you become of things you could do better. This self-awareness is healthy, because it encourages the cultivation of virtues and the shedding of bad habits. And, yes, we all have bad habits.

In Ben Franklin's case, he didn't just review his list occasionally and vow to do better. He knew the folly of trying to cultivate all the virtues at once. So instead, he concentrated each week on a particular virtue. Having thirteen on his list meant he could fit four cycles into one calendar year. He could start the year with a week's worth of focus on temperance, then move on to silence the following week, and so on, and by year's end, he would have devoted a full four weeks to the study of each virtue. In this way, he thought he could advance steadily in the development of his personal character.

My point is not that you should necessarily adopt Franklin's method but understand how it illustrates the tremendous value in working to improve your personal character. As Billy Graham once said, "When wealth is lost, nothing is lost; when health is lost, something is lost; when character is lost, all is lost."

EXERCISE 1: PERSONAL CHARACTER

Using Franklin as inspiration, you can start with my list or create your own list of top personal character traits in both categories of moral and performance traits. Then prepare simple definitions, and get started.

Once you've compiled your list and definitions, give yourself a score of 1 to 10, with 10 being the very best you could do and 1 the worst. Let's say you give yourself a 6 on humility—now write down what you could do differently to improve. Do this with each trait, writing down specific ideas to improve, and then reevaluate every few months. As you give thought to your personal character and to its improvement, I can promise you that six things will happen:

- You will strengthen your personal character.
- Your personal relationships will improve.
- You will do better at work.
- Your self-esteem will rise.
- You will be happier.
- Your chances of personal success will increase.

That's an impressive return on investment in your personal character. So don't shortchange your foundation because everything else depends on it. Take the trouble to make it as solid and strong as possible so that it will support you on your journey.

Chapter 7

THE VALUE OF HARD WORK

"The only thing more important than the will to win is
the will to prepare to win."

—Vince Lombardi

IS THIS THE BEST YOU CAN DO?

When Dr. Henry Kissinger was secretary of state under President Richard
Nixon, he asked one of his staff members to prepare a brief on an urgent
national security issue. He needed a detailed report on the history and
facts involved so he could prepare his recommendations to the president.
This was a top priority, time-sensitive matter, so he chose his smartest staff
member. Dr. Kissinger gave him forty-eight hours to complete the report,
which he received at the deadline. After thanking his staffer for finishing
on time, he put the report in his briefcase and scheduled an 8 a.m. meeting
with the staff member for the next day.

"I only have one question," said Dr. Kissinger at the meeting. "Is this
the best you can do?"

The staffer was caught off balance. "Well, I guess I could have done
some more research and added more specifics to the recommendations,"
he said.

"Okay. Fine. Do that, and give it to me by 6 p.m. today, and we'll meet
again at 8 a.m. tomorrow."

Dr. Kissinger received the report at 6 p.m. and again put it in his brief-case. At 8 the next morning, he again asked, "Is this the best you can do?" The frustrated staffer replied, "I have done more research on the history and sharpened my recommendations. The only thing I may have left out is information on the personalities of the key decision makers."

"Okay. Fine. Do that, and give it to me by 6 p.m. today, and we'll meet again at 8 a.m. tomorrow." When the staffer delivered the report at 6 p.m., Dr. Kissinger asked for the third time: "Is this the best you can do?"

"Absolutely, Dr. Kissinger," he said. "This is the best I can do!" "Good," he said, "Now I'll read it."

Why go through this routine with his most trusted staff member? Because Dr. Kissinger knew that to succeed at his job, he had to be thoroughly prepared to make the best, clearest recommendation possible to the president. He couldn't be confident in his recommendations and his preparation unless the staff member in question had performed the required task to the very best of his ability.

It definitely took more time, but it was worth it. Dr. Kissinger knew that getting the job done *right* would take a lot more effort than just getting the job done. In this case, the final report versus the initial report reflects the difference between doing your job and doing your *best*.

It is almost impossible to do your best on the first try. In my experience, the first time I do something is nothing more than a good start. After I have improved it two or three times, it is starting to approach the best I can do. This takes more time and more effort, but it vastly improves the end product. This is the value of hard work—of putting in that extra effort, of going beyond what is merely required. It is the difference between mediocrity and excellence, and it leads to success. There's no sugar-coating it: Real success begins and ends with hard work.

Hard work is a requirement for success in every worthwhile endeavor. Almost everything in life worth having must be earned, and putting in the hard work is how you earn it. It also increases self-esteem, preparedness, competence, and confidence, all of which are necessary for a successful and happy life. As Zig Ziglar says, "There are no elevators to success. You have to take the stairs."

SOLID GROUND

Others may think hard work is an obvious factor to point out, but when I say hard work, I don't just mean the normal effort between 9 a.m. and 5 p.m., Monday through Friday. Forty hours a week may get you by in your field, but if you really want to be successful, it's going to take at least sixty hours a week of hard work, even if you're blessed with great talent.

WORK HARDER AND SMARTER

"My dear, if you would only recognize that life is hard, things would be much easier for you."

—Supreme Court Justice Louis Brandeis to his daughter

I always chuckle when I hear people say, "Work smarter, not harder." I'm all in favor of finding ways to work more efficiently, but why pretend as if you have a choice? The people who use this catchphrase sound like they're trying to find a shortcut when, in fact, there are none. Anyone who has ever really succeeded will tell you it takes both.

Success, in any area, comes down to how motivated you are—how much time and energy you're willing to invest. People driven to achieve are willing to invest a lot more than those who aren't. No matter what your job is, there will always be more that you can do. If you're a doctor, you can see more patients. If you're a scientist, you can do more research. And if you're in sales, you can make more sales calls. The work is never done. The only real limitation on how hard you're willing to work is you. And it always comes down to how much time you are willing to invest.

Let's look at it as if you are a student. To get good grades in college, you have to go to class and do your homework. How much time you spend on the homework usually determines your grade. If you just go to class, you'll probably get a C. If you just go to class and do your homework, you'll likely get a B. Getting an A, however, takes going to class, doing your homework, plus a lot of extra time and effort outside the classroom.

That's also how jobs are. Going to work from nine to five is like just going to class in college. If that is all you do, you'll do okay but probably not great. I've seen a lot of people, including some with some great natural talent, go through life with a forty-hour-a-week mentality, and they always plateau early in their careers. Talent carries you only so far; so if you lack that drive, you're probably going to stall.

Hard workers, by contrast, set themselves up for success. When times are good, they get promotions. And when times get tough and an organization needs to reduce its staff, who do you think gets laid off? Those who just show up and do the minimum, that's who.

HARD WORK LEADS TO SELF-WORTH

"Hard work is where self-worth and self-esteem begin."

—Unknown

I'll never forget my first real job. It was the summer after my freshman year in college at a pipeline construction company, called D, S & P, in Lexington, Kentucky. They hired me to run a jackhammer and rock drill, and because it was a union company, I was the only guy on the crew allowed to do it. For eight hours a day, all summer long, I used a jackhammer or rock drill to break up rocks and drill holes in solid rock to load and shoot dynamite—all for the hourly rate of $3.18.

This was hard work. I remember waking up every morning stiff and sore, even at the age of nineteen. But because it was so hard and I kept at it all summer, it made me feel very good about myself. Not many kids my age had a job this tough, so I took pride in having the work ethic and stamina to get through it.

That's another major benefit of hard work. It not only helps you meet your goals; it also offers real dignity. Knowing you've put in your best effort, day after day, really elevates your self-esteem in a dramatic way.

You can even use hard work to overcome years of bad programming. None of us, after all, is born with high or low self-esteem. It begins in our childhood and grows or withers based on the feedback we receive from our parents, friends, teachers, and, most importantly, ourselves. The best way to characterize self-esteem is as the tone you use when you talk to yourself (and we all talk to ourselves, even if it's not out loud).

So ask yourself: are you building your self-esteem each day or tearing it down? Hard work can help you become a builder. The satisfaction of a job well done will work wonders for your self-esteem. Self-esteem has nothing to do with what others think of you. It's what *you* think of you. And self-esteem isn't something others can give you through praise, compliments, or attaboys. In fact, unearned praise or flattery is pretty easy to see through and can even reinforce low self-esteem.

You can't build your self-esteem by reading books, taking classes, or by doing easy things. The only real way to build your self-esteem is by actually doing things that are estimable. This includes doing your best and working hard, to be sure, but there are many other ways too. Showing courage, helping others, not taking the easy route, and trying to improve yourself will all move you forward on your journey to better self-esteem.

Deep down, we know whether we've done our best or not. When we delay gratification and sacrifice our fun and enjoyment to do something that is estimable or worthy of esteem, our self-esteem increases. And once we take the time to turn this practice into a habit, higher esteem and self-confidence inevitably follow.

HARD WORK LEADS TO PREPAREDNESS

"Nothing in the world can take the place of persistence. Talent will not. Genius will not. And education will not. Persistence and determination alone are omnipotent."

—Calvin Coolidge

Successful people understand the need to prepare. As Stephen Covey says, "If I had an hour to chop down a tree, I'd spend thirty minutes sharpening my ax!" Why? Because that preparation time—a perfect example of working smarter and harder—improves your knowledge, your skills, and your stamina, which all increase your odds for success. Psychologists who have studied successful people in all walks of life have discovered a pattern to this preparation. They call it deliberate practice.

Deliberate practice means having a regular, structured routine (usually daily) where you set aside time to "sharpen your saw," do your homework, set goals, and prepare for your day. Spending this concentrated time in preparation enables you to be more thoughtful, consider more options, enjoy better focus, and be better prepared. And as you become better prepared, you become more competent, and therefore, more confident.

HARD WORK LEADS TO COMPETENCE

"Hard work leads to competence. Competence leads to confidence. It takes confidence to succeed and it all starts with hard work."

—Rick Pitino

I had a friend in high school named Doug Flynn. Doug was a year behind me in school and played on the Bryan Station High School football and baseball teams. As a junior, he was about 5'6" and weighed 120 pounds. Because of his size, Doug didn't get much playing time. But he was always at practice and was a decent athlete. As a senior on the baseball team, he finally won a starting job at second base.

After graduation, he made the baseball team at the University of Kentucky as a walk-on but rarely played. Undeterred, he kept practicing. By his senior year, Doug was UK's starting second baseman and had grown to six feet tall. He had become a very good college baseball player—so good, in fact, that he tried out for the Cincinnati Reds during their glory years in the 1970s when they were known as the Big Red Machine.

Doug's hard work was starting to pay off. The Reds signed him to a contract in 1971, and after honing his craft in the minor leagues for five years, he made the major league team in 1975. Doug became their top utility infielder and backed up the legendary Reds' starting infield of Joe Morgan at second base, Dave Concepción at shortstop, and Pete Rose at third base. He went on to have a successful, eleven-year professional baseball career spent primarily with Cincinnati, the New York Mets, and the Montreal Expos.

SOLID GROUND

Was Doug Flynn a born athlete? Far from it. He *made* himself one. After years of practice and continual improvement at each level of baseball, Doug became an accomplished athlete. He gained his success the old-fashioned way—by earning it. An important principle embedded in the story of Doug Flynn is that his success didn't come quickly or easily. It rarely does. Hard work always precedes competence, which precedes success.

Many times, when we see successful people in sports, business, medicine, or anywhere, we wrongly conclude their talent or their brilliance is a gift. Sometimes we even envy them and wish we were so talented. Yet very few of these people see their success as a gift. They will instead credit the hard work, the sacrifice, the preparation, and the determination that preceded their success and made it possible.

James Allen wrote that envious people sometimes consider the successful to be lucky:

> They do not see the trials and failures and struggles which these men have voluntarily encountered in order to gain their experience; have no knowledge of the sacrifices they have made, of the undaunted efforts they have put forth, of the faith they have exercised, that they might overcome the apparently insurmountable, and realize the Vision of their heart. They do not know the darkness and the heartaches; they only see the light and joy and call it 'luck.' They do not see the long and arduous journey, but only behold the pleasant goal, and call it 'good fortune.'

It takes hard work to achieve. And it's a step-by-step rather than a leaps-and-bounds process. Once I talked with a sports psychologist about using sports as a model for business improvement, and he invited me to play a round of golf with him. His theory was that each golf shot is independent of every other shot, and that most golfers get upset when they hit a bad shot and try to make up for it on the next one. His advice was to set a simple goal on each stroke to hit a small target, and consider that single stroke as a success if you hit your target. The only important shot in golf is the next one.

He then described how self-confidence works. We all have a self-confidence comfort zone. On a scale of 1 to 10, let's say your self-confidence range is 6 to 8. If things get below 6, you are not comfortable, so you naturally begin to do what you can to get back into your comfort zone. But if things get too good and you are a 9, you begin to undermine yourself. Why? Because you don't think you deserve it. By working harder and getting better, you can actually move your comfort zone up so that when great opportunities occur, you are mentally ready to seize them.

You've no doubt noticed that I like to use sports metaphors. The central elements of competition and self-improvement are what link sports with success in any field. There are techniques one must learn to perform at a high level, whether as an offensive lineman or an accountant. Sports are like life except that all the ups and downs, triumphs and adversities, play out in sixty minutes or nine innings rather than over the course of a lifetime.

EMBRACING THE STRUGGLE

"Strength and courage aren't always measured in medals and victories. The strongest people aren't always the people who win, but the people who don't give up when they lose."

—Ashley Hodgeson

A few years ago, I met with David Blanchard, the cofounder of a nonprofit called Praxis. Praxis identifies, trains, and supports faith-based entrepreneurs in their twenties and thirties. Its mission is to help these young entrepreneurs improve the world, and the Praxis model for success is simple yet profound. It involves only three steps:

- The Vision
- The Struggle
- The Journey

In hindsight, that is exactly the way it worked for me and will probably work for you. In my case, the vision wasn't fully formed until my late thirties. The struggle was from about forty to fifty, and the journey was everything after that. In his book *The 10X Rule: The Only Difference Between Success and Failure* (2011), Grant Cardone makes the simple point that just about everything worth doing takes ten times the effort you think it will take.

The big takeaway here is that you just can't avoid the struggle. Nothing worth doing comes easy, so you should expect and be prepared for a struggle of some kind. This struggle will always require more hard work, persistence, and resilience than you expect. Only if you are conditioned for the hard work and have practiced persistence and built up your resilience muscles will you be able to survive the struggle phase and complete the journey of your dreams.

CONTINUOUS IMPROVEMENT

"I have not failed. I have just found 10,000 ways that will not work."

—Thomas Edison

As the owner and CEO of a homebuilding company committed to quality, I spent a lot of time studying how my company could deliver error-free homes every time. The average home took about six months to build, and for twenty years we averaged about one home per day.

While reading up on the subject of quality, I ran across the Japanese word *kaizan*, which is their primary principle for creating quality products. *Kaizan* simply means continuous improvement. When you reach one level of achievement, you don't rest on your laurels—you look for ways to get even better. It's a process of seeking perfection, and it is continuous and never-ending.

At T.W. Lewis Company, we got serious about quality improvement in 1995, and by 2005, we were consistently delivering exceptional homes. It took ten hard years of trial, error, experimentation, failure, adjustment, and improvement before we really got our system working. It took many, many small steps to cover all the different components involved. In business and in life, it takes strategy and execution to succeed. Strategy is the big picture, and execution lies in the details. Strategy is important and necessary but not sufficient. Execution is the hard part.

DON'T BE INVOLVED, BE COMMITTED

"You can win 80 percent of the time if you just show up, 90 percent of the time if you show up with a plan, and 100 percent of the time if you show up with a plan and commit."

—Woody Allen

Success begins with commitment, one of those really important concepts people often overlook. It's easy to stand by a goal when it's new and your will hasn't been tested, but can you continue to do so day in and day out? Even when you're tired and discouraged? That's the difference between those who succeed and those who don't.

When I started my company in 1991, after leaving Trammell Crow Residential, I was 100 percent committed. To this day, I can still remember the confidence I had in knowing that none of my many competitors could possibly match the level of hard work and commitment I was willing to invest.

Commitment means there's no turning back. You can't quit, because you're in it for the long haul. A lot of good things begin to happen once you're committed—things that would never have happened otherwise. Once you're fully committed, you have to find solutions to the difficulties you will face. It's an attitude that fuels your persistence and strengthens your resiliency, making success possible.

Relatively few people realize the power of commitment. I know a lot of very bright and talented people who were never sure about what they wanted to do, so they stayed on the fence. They kept their options open, never taking any risks or committing themselves to anything. As Theodore Roosevelt once said, "They live in the gray twilight that knows neither victory nor defeat." And that's not the best place to live. Committing is the hardest part of success. After that, it gets easier.

SOLID GROUND

THANK GOODNESS IT'S MONDAY

"The more I want to get something done, the less I call it work."

—Richard Bach

I have always found fun in working and pursuing a goal. Believe it or not, when you set goals that you really want to achieve and that inspire you, working toward them doesn't seem like work. That has been my mindset for as long as I can remember, and most successful people share it. Successful people love to work, so they do it a lot. Their mindset is the grindset, and they love the grind.

I used to have a sales manager who didn't think this way. On Fridays, he'd always say, "Happy Friday." A lot of people feel that way, but I never liked that phrase because it implies that happiness can only occur outside of work—as if his job is some kind of prison from which he is released for the weekend. And then on Mondays, this sales manager always asked, "How was your weekend?" Maybe he was just trying to make conversation, but the mindset behind that question always rankled me.

Many people live for the weekend. They spend Monday through Friday planning for it. There was even a hit song in the 1980s called "Working for the Weekend." Don't get me wrong: It's certainly good to recharge your batteries on your days off, but if you focus too much on your weekends, you'll likely have many great weekends and little else.

I've conducted a lot of college scholarship interviews over the years, and my favorite question to ask these sharp high school seniors is, "How important is career success to you?" Some will say, "Very important." Some will even say, "It is everything." But I've been shocked that many say, "Well, it's kind of important, but it's not so important that I would sacrifice my happiness for it."

In my experience, happiness and success are two completely different things. To oversimplify, happiness is the natural result of learning and growing as a person and helping others. Success is the result of hard work, talent, persistence, and continuous improvement. This means we all have four options:

- Be unsuccessful and unhappy.
- Be successful but not happy.
- Be happy but not successful.
- Be happy and successful.

Because happiness and success are unrelated, they should be understood and pursued separately. Then you can achieve both!

PERSISTENCE AND RESILIENCE

"Don't run out of breath before you win."

—Derek Anderson

If you're not a basketball fan, you've probably never heard of Derek Anderson. But he can certainly teach us all about the values of persistence and resilience. One of the star players on the 1996–1997 University of Kentucky basketball team, Derek suffered a severe ankle sprain early in the 1997 NCAA tournament that probably cost the team another national championship. This might have discouraged a lesser individual, but Derek had already endured an extremely difficult childhood, which had forced him to grow up early and learn resilience and toughness. Circumstances that cause other people to give up didn't stop Derek, as he noted in his autobiography *Stamina: Don't Run Out of Breath Before You Win* (2013). Moving around in the public housing projects of Louisville, Kentucky, Derek watched his family suffer from the effects of drugs, homelessness, and extreme violence.

But Derek had a gift for basketball that he improved through persistence and hard work. He won a national championship at UK in 1996 and went on to an eleven-year NBA career, winning a championship with the Miami Heat in 2006. He retired from basketball in 2008, but he wasn't one to rest on his laurels. He has since dedicated his life to inspiring and motivating others who come from similar circumstances.

Resiliency is the ability to recover quickly and fully from adversity and hardship. Like persistence, a person's resilience gets stronger the more it is employed. In his book *Toughness: Developing True Strength On and Off the Court* (2013), former Duke basketball star and ESPN analyst Jay Bilas describes toughness as the ability to bend without breaking. It's not a physical trait, but a mental one. No one is born tough or resilient. Both of these skills come through adversity and hard work.

Recent psychological studies on persistence and resilience have concluded that these traits are like a muscle, getting stronger the more they are used. The more you fall down and get up, the more you face difficulties and persist, the stronger your "resilience muscle" becomes. Like all good habits, persistence and resilience take practice and repetition.

Delaying gratification can be quite a challenge in a world that expects and encourages instant gratification. It creates some discomfort, especially when we're not used to telling ourselves *no*. But it's all part of growing up— or it should be. After all, when babies are uncomfortable, they cry. Adults, however, should learn to get comfortable being uncomfortable.

Self-discipline may not sound like fun, but it's essential for success. If you get your way all the time, you will never need to persist. Not getting our way creates the need for persistence and allows us to build this skill.

I believe kids who are taught to work, earn what they receive, and deal with some age-appropriate adversity are much better prepared for dealing with the unavoidable obstacles of life. As parents, we want our children to be strong, so helping them build their persistence and resilience muscles is one of the best gifts we can give them.

MANAGING TIME

Because time is so important, we can't waste it. Over the years, I have learned two simple models that will help you make the most of your time. The Harvard Business School has developed many 2x2 matrices. One of the best is separating our priorities into important and urgent. The matrix— which should be familiar to anyone who has read Stephen Covey's *The 7 Habits of Highly Effective People*—looks like this:

	Important	Not Important
Urgent	Priority #1	Priority #3
Not Urgent	Priority #2	Priority #4

Urgent and Important

The difficulty in managing time is that we are so often overwhelmed with things that are *urgent* (which typically matter to other people), so we rarely get to do things that are *important* (which typically matter to us). Yet the only way we can put ourselves on the path to personal success is to make ourselves spend more time on tasks that are important and less time on tasks that are urgent.

It takes self-discipline to do that. Bosses and colleagues often besiege us with urgent but (to us) unimportant matters. And let's face it: If we show up to work every day with no plan, no vision, and no commitment to hard work, we can easily spend all day, every day, just doing those *urgent* things. We're busy, but we're not moving toward our goals. Your odds of success are much better when you spend your time on things that are important and are aligned with your goals.

Another model for time management involves separating your sphere of concern from your sphere of control. We all naturally gravitate to things that interest us, but we have no influence over most of them. Although our sphere of concern is much bigger than our sphere of control, our time is much better spent on things we can actually control.

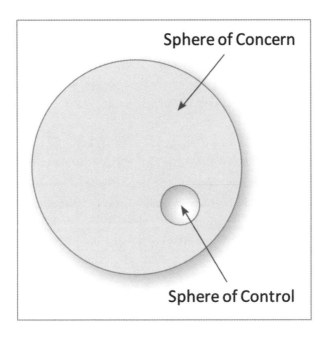

Spheres of Concern and Control

The sphere of concern includes keeping up with our social media, reading the news, and following local, national, or global issues. These things are interesting, and we care about them, but there is not much we can actually do about them. In the sphere of concern, we are only spectators. Our sphere of control, on the other hand, is limited to those things we can actually influence. This includes our job, our personal relationships, our faith, our health, and all other personal responsibilities.

Successful people spend their time on things that are important and are in their sphere of control.

T.W. LEWIS

THE CLOCK IS TICKING

"Most people that get ahead do so with the time that others waste."

—Unknown

Tiger Woods started playing golf at age three. Bill Gates spent all day on a computer in the early 1970s while in high school. Elite NHL hockey players in Canada join special developmental teams as early as age ten. *Time matters.*

In her book *The Defining Decade: Why Your Twenties Matter—And How to Make the Most of Them Now* (2012), Dr. Meg Jay describes a mindset that many millennials have today—the trendy belief that "thirty is the new twenty." In other words, it's okay to goof off and have fun in your twenties, then buckle down and get going in your thirties. Dr. Jay debunks this myth and demonstrates that your twenties are actually your defining decade, one critical to building the foundation of success. I couldn't agree more.

The problem with getting a late start on your career, your job experiences, and your skill development is competition. Once you are out of school, no matter your field, you will be competing with people who are close to you in age. The ones who start early, work hard, and stay late will get way ahead, and they keep progressing. If you start late, you will probably never catch up. And if you postpone the struggle, you're postponing your success. That's why your twenties are so important.

It's in early adulthood that you have the time and opportunity to develop your skills, work toward self-improvement, and learn from failures. These timely investments in your success will certainly pay off later.

The clock is ticking.

Chapter 8

THE MAGIC OF GOAL SETTING

"If you want your dream to come true,
you first have to have a dream."

—T.W. Lewis

Many people fail because they never give themselves a chance. They make the mistake of believing their destiny is controlled by fate, other people, or some forces beyond their control. We can't help where we start in life, and we all will have obstacles to overcome—some of them quite difficult. But how we prosper and where we end up, I'm happy to say, is mostly up to us.

From a very young age, I have believed in what I call deliberate living. By this, I mean being in charge of your own life, consciously deciding what path you want to take, and then having the courage and persistence to take it. Henry David Thoreau, one of the great American philosophers, expressed it well in *Walden* (1854): "If one advances confidently in the direction of his dreams, and endeavors to live the life which he has imagined, he will meet with a success unexpected in common hours."

My father initially introduced me to this way of thinking when he made me memorize William Ernest Henley's short poem "Invictus." Its last four lines made a lasting impression.

> It matters not how strait the gate
> How charged with punishment the scroll.
> I am the master of my fate,
> I am the captain of my soul.

This poem resonated with me immediately. We're not puppets; we're the ones in charge of our lives. But to be good "captains," we need to be fully responsible and accountable for our actions.

So what does a good ship captain do? He first determines his destination. That allows him to set a sensible course to follow—one that will maximize his chances of arriving as safely and quickly as possible. Then he makes sure his ship is in good order and fully stocked for the journey. And he sets sail. Once we know where we want to go, we can overcome the crosswinds and obstacles that stand in our way.

I have always gotten a lot of joy out of setting goals. And they have changed over the years: Make a million dollars. Be a loving husband. Be a great father. Be a strong Christian. Get my handicap below ten in golf. Obviously not every goal carries the same weight, but if it's a goal that inspires me, it helps clear the clutter so I can concentrate on what I want to accomplish.

I usually write down my goals every month, and, as circumstances change, I reset them. Some stick, some don't, and they're not chiseled in stone. They are meant to be reevaluated. Set, evaluate, reset. Some people set their goals on New Year's Day and assess their progress annually on December 31. This is better than nothing, but it doesn't work. It is far better to assess your progress much more frequently.

Something magical happens when you set a goal that you really want to achieve. It inspires you to become your best self; it focuses and releases your energy, and it directs your efforts in the direction of your dreams.

SMART OR HARD?

"A goal is a dream with a deadline."

—Napoleon Hill

Although everyone would agree it's important to have goals, expressing them in the best way is an art. The wrong kind of goals can actually impede our progress or discourage us. Two popular acronyms have cropped up over the past thirty years or so to address this problem in goal setting. The first are the so-called SMART goals:

- **S** Specific
- **M** Measurable
- **A** Achievable
- **R** Realistic
- **T** Timely

This model, developed in the early 1980s, really caught on, and it's easy to see why. It's an efficient way to look at both business and personal goals, and it can help you sharpen them into something achievable. And no one wants to argue with the word *smart*. But it's incomplete. It addresses the "head" but ignores the role of the "heart," or personal inspiration.

More recently, Mark Murphy, CEO of Leadership IQ, introduced a second acronym—one that's more emotional and a bit less rational called HARD goals:

- **H** Heartfelt
- **A** Animated
- **R** Required
- **D** Difficult

Although both the SMART and HARD models offer good general guidance, neither model fully captures the central role of goal setting in shaping a successful life. From my experience, I would include some additional dimensions for setting your goals.

YOUR GOALS SHOULD INSPIRE YOU

"The value of setting goals is not so much what we achieve, but what we become in the process."

—Unknown

Your goals shouldn't simply lay out a series of milestones you hope to achieve. To begin, you need to dig deeper and create an overall vision for the person you want to become. To do this, you'll want to take these five important categories into account, because they are the primary areas where you can find the most meaning and purpose in life:

- Personal Growth
- Family
- Career
- Community
- Faith

All your goals should inspire you, which is why it's so important to consider the whole person. Goals should get you excited about becoming the best person you can be in the areas that matter most to you. If your goals don't excite and inspire you, set new ones.

It's also important that your goals be authentic. They should reflect your personal history, who you are now, and who you want to become, not who others want you to be.

SOLID GROUND

My acronym for setting goals uses the word inspire:

I	Inspiring.	To be truly motivated, you need to be personally inspired.
N	Noble.	Select goals grounded in your highest moral principles.
S	Specific.	The more detailed a goal is, the better. Don't be vague.
P	Personal.	An authentic goal will align with your strongest values.
I	Immediate.	Think about what you can start doing now.
R	Realistic.	Reach high, but set goals you know can be achieved.
E	Expected.	Make clear what you expect of yourself, and commit.

I have learned that it is better to focus on the quality of what you want to become rather than just the quantity that's involved in getting there. I call these "become goals." For example, instead of saying you want to lose ten pounds, say you want to become a person who eats healthy and is in great shape. Or instead of saying you want to earn $100,000 in income this year, set a goal to become the best salesperson in your company.

It goes back to Dale Carnegie and those lessons I learned in Dayton. Appeal to your own nobler motives. That's how you inspire yourself. If I say, "I want to make a million dollars," that's not appealing to a nobler motive. But if I say, "I want to become the best homebuilder in America," that's an inspiring goal. That's uplifting, personal, and authentic.

Deciding on your goals also teaches you what your goals are *not*. Knowing what you want helps you figure out what you don't want. If your goal is to be a great husband and father and be financially independent, and your friend calls and says, "Hey, let's go to Mexico and lie on the beach," you'll know that's what you don't want.

THINK. RETHINK.

"If you keep on doing what you've always done, you will keep on getting what you've always got."

—Unknown

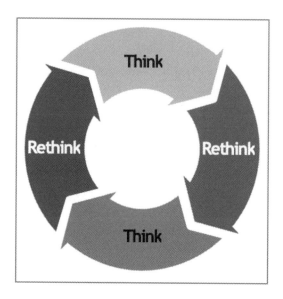

Think/Rethink

One of the techniques I have long used in goal setting is to write things down. A dream or a goal can't become real if it never leaves your head, and the process of putting pen to paper can actually help you figure out exactly what you want to do.

The very process of turning your vague thoughts into specific words and putting them down for future reference can help shape your actions to achieve them. Seeing them in writing can give them a life of their own.

I started doing this in grad school. Whether it was goals, problems, or plans, I liked to write them down. Once I did this, I could then look at them and ask, "What can I do to make this better?" or "What am I missing?" Then I would revise it. And then revise it again. After three or four iterations of thinking and rethinking, I would end up with something that was more clear, more inspirational, and more actionable. This process also helped me become more invested in the plan and the goal, and encouraged me to confidently proceed.

USE MULTIPLE TIME FRAMES

"A man without a goal is like a ship without a rudder."

—Thomas Carlyle

I have also learned it is best to set goals for several different time frames. My favorites are:

- Daily
- Monthly
- Annually
- Someday

Daily goals are important because they emphasize the importance of today. Monthly and annual goals are good because they help you focus on what is really important versus urgent. Someday goals are really great because they become your North Star and will keep you focused on your dreams. I would suggest using only the five most important goals in each category. Using different time frames for your goals can also help motivate you to work toward them steadily.

No goal has to be permanent. Sometimes giving up or changing a goal is the best decision. Use your judgment. Those someday goals can also shape your immediate activities. Whether your someday goal is living on a farm and fishing every day or owning your own company, it will be a hint as to what you should be doing *today*.

SETTING GOALS LEADS TO PASSION

"To avoid criticism, say nothing, do nothing, be nothing."

—Aristotle

I roll my eyes when I hear someone tell a young person, "Just follow your passion, and everything else will work out." That's nonsense. We hear a lot these days about finding our passion, but the word *passion* is used differently today than in the past. Improperly understood, it can set you up for failure.

Passion comes from the Greek word *pathos*, which means suffering. Having passion originally meant caring about something so much you were willing to suffer for it. Good examples of this are the Passion of Christ or the passion that parents have for their children. Because good parents have invested so much time and energy in their children, love them deeply, and have sacrificed and suffered for them, they become passionate about them. But that passion doesn't come instantly; you don't have the same feeling the day a child is born that you will once he or she is grown up. You love your child, of course, but the real passion of parenting comes after years of suffering (trust me on this one).

Was it my passion at nineteen to build houses? No. Did I suffer in becoming a homebuilder? Yes. Not everyone knows at age twenty or even age forty what their passion in life is going to be. It's still developing, and it changes over time. What I care about today is not the same thing I cared about as a young man. To expect a teenager to figure out what his passion is and set a life course based on his feelings at that moment is ridiculous.

Passion develops over the course of a journey in which you are fully invested. Setting a goal is the first step in this journey, and passion follows. Psychological studies have shown there are definable steps that lead to passion:

- Step 1. You start with a clear goal.

- Step 2. The goal creates personal excitement that releases energy and fuels action.

- Step 3. The investment of personal time and energy creates progress toward the goal.

- Step 4. Over time, the persistent investment of time and energy creates the commitment that is needed to overcome the obstacles, and you achieve the goal.

- Step 5. The struggle of overcoming the obstacles leads to deep personal satisfaction and joy.

- Step 6. This satisfaction and joy become passion.

In other words, finding passion takes time, and it comes at the end, not the beginning. During our lives, we will have many different passions, and they will usually start with setting a goal.

HAVE A DREAM

"Hope is not a plan."

—Jimmy Dykes

Having a dream means having goals. And those goals need to be as clear as possible—and in writing. I can remember doing this when I was at the very beginning of my career, at age twenty-three, in my second year in grad school at UNC. On a six-by-eight-inch piece of paper, I wrote down my career dream:

Start my own company by age thirty in the construction/development business, and make it prosper. Founding principles will be:

- Quality product—energy efficient, ecologically sound
- Service to customers
- Growth and opportunity for employees
- Profitability

I still have this handwritten note. It might seem simple, but it was all the inspiration I needed at the time. Having this simple and clear goal was the first step in achieving career success for me—and it can work for you too. The clearer you can make your dream, the better. So write it down—and commit to it.

EXERCISE 2: PERSONAL GOALS

Now it's time to get started getting clear on your own dreams.
Use this format as a way to set clear goals:

	DAILY	MONTHLY	ANNUAL	SOMEDAY
PERSONAL	· · · · ·	· · · · ·	· · · · ·	· · · · ·
FAMILY	· · · · ·	· · · · ·	· · · · ·	· · · · ·
CAREER	· · · · ·	· · · · ·	· · · · ·	· · · · ·
COMMUNITY	· · · · ·	· · · · ·	· · · · ·	· · · · ·
FAITH	· · · · ·	· · · · ·	· · · · ·	· · · · ·

Chapter 9

THE BENEFITS OF SELF-AWARENESS

"I try my best to be just like I am,
but everybody wants you to be just like them."

—Bob Dylan, "Maggie's Farm"

L et's take a step back in this chapter and get into something even more fundamental. We've talked about the importance of personal character, of hard work, and of setting goals for where we want to go. Now let's consider something even more basic and just as important: self-awareness.

Why is this so important? Because each one of us is unique and complex. What works for me won't necessarily work for you, and vice versa. The sooner you understand yourself and what makes you tick, the further you'll go in life. "No problem there," you may think. "I know all about myself." But do you really?

It's logical to assume you do. After all, nobody spends more time with you than you do. You've had a front-row seat at every thought, word, and action of your life. But as most psychologists can tell you, human beings are very skilled at self-deception. Our minds are constantly playing up what we want to believe about ourselves and filtering out what we don't want to believe—and they usually do so automatically without us even realizing it.

"Your backstage access to your own mind sometimes makes you the last person on Earth others should trust about it," Adam Grant, a professor of management and psychology at the University of Pennsylvania's Wharton School of Business, writes in *The Atlantic*. "Think of it like owning a car: Just because you've driven it for years doesn't mean you can pinpoint when and why the engine broke down."

Besides, most of us are busy. Day after day, we do our jobs and stay on top of a dozen other tasks. The little free time we get is devoted to fun activities with family and friends or to our own hobbies. How much time do we actually devote to understanding ourselves? To assessing our strengths and weaknesses? For most of us, the honest answer is not much.

Maybe you have done something in this area: read a book, taken a test, gone on a retreat. That's fine, but self-awareness isn't a one-time activity. It's not something you do once and then you're done. Self-awareness is an ongoing process—or at least it should be.

Take me. I've done pretty well in my life. Why? Is it the result of hard work, talent, or luck? Was it my dad's bankruptcy, which taught me not to waste things and gave me the drive to succeed? It's some measure of all these things, of course, but it's more than that. I believe I reached my goals primarily because my strengths, motivating values, and my behavioral style were very well-matched with my career path. This made going to work every day feel natural and exciting, so I loved to work. Because I enjoyed it, I did a lot of it and became very good at my job.

What if Michael Jordan tried to succeed as a baseball player (which he did in 1994; he hit .202 for the minor-league Birmingham Barons) or Bill Gates became a schoolteacher? My point here is that you can be happy and successful doing a lot of different things, but you can only reach your full potential if you engage your natural strengths and your motivating values. And this takes self-awareness.

Self-awareness means consciously knowing your strengths, your weaknesses, your personality traits, and your values. Becoming more aware of these qualities leads to better self-acceptance, better personal and career decisions, and ulti-mately to becoming a more successful and authentic person.

Self-awareness also takes effort. Dealing with the complexity of today's world isn't easy. Finding the right path is difficult, and the social pressure to conform is intense. It's tempting to just go with the flow. But if you really want to succeed, you have to resist. Increasing your sense of self-awareness, the knowledge of who you are at your core—what you're naturally good at, what you're not, and how you can improve—can help you cut a better path through the challenges you'll face.

But learning this takes time. Self-awareness is best achieved by expos-ing ourselves to multiple experiences, responsibilities, and adversity. Most of us gain some awareness of what we're good at and what we're not simply by going to school and working. But there are many assessment tools readi-ly available to help us do this. Learning and appreciating your unique traits and then following your values and strengths will give you the best chance of long-term success in both life and career. And it will also lead to much better decision making.

WHY SELF-AWARENESS MATTERS

"The unexamined life is not worth living."

—Socrates

Years ago, members of the faculty of one of the best business schools in the world, conducted a research project of successful CEOs to find out what they believed was the most important quality of successful people. Was it intelligence? Analytical skills? People skills? It was none of those. Their conclusion: self-awareness.

This really got me thinking, and then it hit me: people who are self-aware use their strengths to get ahead and find others to shore up their weak-nesses. And that's a big deal! Self-awareness has a lot of tangible benefits.

SELF-AWARENESS LEADS TO SELF-ACCEPTANCE

"Don't care too much about what others think about you,
but act in ways that make you proud."

—Dennis Prager

Everyone has an opinion, and when you ask someone for his or her advice, you're getting advice grounded in that other person's values. How much do you know about him? How much does he know about you? His values may be completely contrary to yours. But he thinks you are just like him and that you will act the way he would act in your situation. You can get pulled off course this way or stumble over unnecessary doubts.

Because none of us is completely satisfied with ourself, we often have self-doubts, and these can undermine our success. But self-acceptance enables us to increase our confidence and our chances for success. Once we're clear on who we are, we get more comfortable in our own skin, accept our flaws, and become more self-accepting.

SELF-AWARENESS IDENTIFIES YOUR BIASES

"Know thyself."

—Socrates

Knowing your biases is another big advantage. Once you're clear on your behavioral style and what motivates you, you can make allowance for your biases, which are the "default settings" that you use to discount the behaviors and motivators you don't have. For example, I have a tendency to see everything as a problem that needs fixing. This can be a great strength, but it is also a weakness. Being aware of this tendency and moderating my behavior when needed helps me get along better with others at home and at work.

SELF-AWARENESS HELPS YOU IDENTIFY YOUR STRENGTHS

"Too many people overvalue what they are not and undervalue what they are."

—Malcolm Forbes

Several years ago, I went to a behind-the-scenes event put on by our local NBA team, the Phoenix Suns. The team owners were showing a group of businesspeople how they used analytics to win basketball games. I was sitting next to their general manager and had just read Michael Lewis' *Moneyball: The Art of Winning an Unfair Game* (2003), a very entertaining account of how the Oakland A's then-general manager, Billy Beane, used data analytics to discover the most important statistics in baseball.

It turns out that home runs, base hits, and RBIs are important, but not as important as a player's on-base percentage. This discovery led to finding overlooked, undervalued players who would win more games for less money spent on payroll—a big discovery.

So I asked the Suns' GM, "What's the most important statistic in the NBA?" Without hesitation, he said, "Shot selection." He explained: "All these players are extremely talented, but each one has a special strength. Some are great three-point shooters, others do best at midrange jump shots, and some are best at just taking it to the rim."

Coaches advise players to take only their best shots, not their low-percentage shots. The more the whole team does this, the more they win. In other words, the players are aware of their strengths and weaknesses, and they use their strengths to win.

SELF-AWARENESS TOOLS

"The challenge is not simply to survive. Hell, anyone can do that. It's to survive as yourself, undiminished."

—Elia Kazan

Today, the personality-assessment industry is thriving. Almost all large corporations use some type of assessment tool in recruitment to help match people and jobs. But some academics are skeptical of the value of these tests. They think such assessments put people in boxes or fail to account for the complexity of human personality. Of course, people are complicated and unique, but I have found these tools extremely useful, both for myself and for many others because they help us understand our strengths and weaknesses.

Since my days in Chapel Hill in Dr. Gerry Bell's class, I have explored and used many of these tools. My favorites include Myers-Briggs, Disc, and Indigo.

Myers-Briggs—Knowing Your Temperament

Probably the most well known of the self-assessment instruments is the Myers-Briggs Type Indicator (MBTI) test. Created by Isabel Briggs Myers and her mother, Katharine Briggs, in the 1940s, the assessment is based on the work of psychologist Carl G. Jung, a contemporary of Sigmund Freud and one of the most significant thought leaders of twentieth-century psychology.

The Myers-Briggs test essentially uses a personality inventory to translate Jung's theories about personality types into a format generally understandable and useful in everyday life. It identifies and describes sixteen distinct temperaments based on the preferences of perception and judgment established by Jung. According to the MBTI, these types include sixteen combinations of the core preferences: Extraversion or Introversion, Sensing or Intuition, Thinking or Feeling, Judging or Perceiving.

The Myers-Briggs assessment has proved to be very popular. It has been used by millions of people and many corporations like McKinsey, General Motors, and Procter & Gamble to make hiring decisions and ensure they have the right people in the right positions.

Over the years, I have used the Myers-Briggs within my organization as well to help guide the process of hiring. Basically, the Myers-Briggs answers four critical questions:

- How do you get your energy—from being alone or around others? (Introversion or Extraversion)

- How do you take in information? Do you pay more attention to facts or intuition? (Sensing or Intuition)

- Do you make your decisions with your head or your heart? (Thinking or Feeling)

- Are you planned and organized or spontaneous? (Judging or Perceiving)

In reality, of course, each of us tends to fall somewhere in the middle on each scale. For example, on a scale of 1 to 10 for the Introvert/Extravert, you may be a 4 (leaning more toward Introvert) or a 9 (a strong Extrovert).

Once you know your Myers-Briggs type, you can use it to identify opportunities for personal growth and development. Knowing that you tend to be more introverted or extroverted, more factual or intuitive, more thinking or feeling, or more judging or perceiving, can really help you get along better with others and manage yourself. It can also help you understand your biases.

But the Myers-Briggs test has its limitations. People don't neatly fit into only sixteen types. We are more complex and need a lot more categories. Also, it only measures temperament, not strengths or values. That's where some other tests can prove useful.

DISC—How You Act

The most popular assessment for building self-awareness is the DISC—an acronym for Dominance, Influence, Steadiness, and Compliance—which was created by Harvard graduate and Tufts University professor William Moulton Marston in his book *Emotions of Normal People*, published in 1928. Marston, a teacher and psychologist who also felt Jung's influence, was the inventor of the lie detector test.

Marston developed the DISC theory as a way to determine how people tend to behave under different conditions or environments. DISC was based on observational behaviors, thus making it more objective and descriptive. Various versions of DISC assessments are available today. Here are the basic tenets:

- Dominance. How people deal with problems and challenges.
- Influence. How people deal with people and contacts.
- Steadiness. How people handle pace and change.
- Compliance. How people respond to procedures and constraints.

Modern DISC theory acknowledges that most people have a measure of each core DISC behavioral style. But the styles are present in various combinations for each person. While most people have a primary style, the DISC assessment measures both your natural style *and* your adapted style to reflect how you are trying to modify your natural behavior.

Indigo—Combining Behaviors, Motivations, and Skills

Indigo is a comprehensive assessment that evolved from the work of the late Bill Bonnstetter, a Phoenix-based friend and role model of mine with over forty years of experience in studying people and their potential.

Indigo starts with the basic DISC assessment but adds motivating values and skills. Bonnstetter based his first assessments in the late 1970s on Marston's work, and then refined them through his in-depth research. Bill became a major contributor to the evolution and perfection of DISC theory, especially in the area of motivating values, basing much of his analysis on German philosopher and psychologist Eduard Spranger's book *Types of Men: The Psychology and Ethics of Personality*, which was published in English in 1928. Incorporating these powerful motivating values was a big step toward better understanding our most fundamental motives.

MOTIVATING VALUES

"Be yourself. Everyone else is already taken."

—Unknown

My favorite part of the Indigo assessment is the motivating values because it explains so much about why we do what we do. These are different from the core values that I discuss later and are very important when it comes to selecting a career path. These characteristics represent your worldview and strongly influence your decisions in every aspect of your life. Just as there are three primary colors (red, blue, and yellow), there are six primary motivating values:

- Theoretical. Those who value knowledge for knowledge's sake, continuing education, and intellectual growth.

- Utilitarian. Those who value practical accomplishments, results, and rewards for their investments of time, resources, and energy.

- Aesthetic. Those who value balance in their lives, creative self-expression, beauty, and nature.

- Social. Those who value opportunities to be of service to others and contribute to the progress and well-being of society.

- Individualistic. Those who value personal recognition, freedom, and control over their own destiny.

- Traditional. Those who value traditions inherent in social structure, rules, regulations, and principles.

The Indigo is the most comprehensive assessment I've seen. Once I learned about it, I began using it in my business, with friends, and in awarding scholarships to college students. Since you are reading this book, please accept my invitation to take this assessment. It will take about forty-five minutes to complete, and the report will be emailed to you within minutes of completion. Just go to: **www.ttisurvey.com** and enter your response link: **383191LGX**.

Remember, however, to take all these assessments with a grain of salt. There are few absolutes when it comes to understanding people. No assessment can really capture the depth and entirety of a human being. But this kind of data is great information to have as you seek better understanding of yourself and others.

CORE VALUES

Core values, the second kind of personal values, are the ones that define the kind of person you respect and want to become. Several years ago, I created a core values exercise that I have given to prospective employees as well as scholarship applicants. In this exercise, I list 100 different core values and ask each person to identify his top twenty-five, then top twelve, and finally his top six core values.

I've personally gone through this exercise many times over the past decade, and each time I come up with the same results:

- Honesty
- Integrity
- Hard work
- Reliability
- Compassion
- Achievement

Although all 100 of these values are positive, even praiseworthy, no one can feel equally strong about all of them. Selecting certain values that are more important than others is a good way to get you to think critically about what matters most to *you*. It forces you to make some tough choices, but that's really what values are all about. Once you go through the exercise and know your top six core values, you can better align your decisions with them.

Knowing your values will clarify what you stand for as well as what you won't stand for. Sometimes knowing when to say *no* is more important than knowing when to say *yes*. Understanding your boundaries also creates a lot of freedom within them and takes some of the stress out of making important decisions.

EXERCISE 3: CORE VALUES

Below is a list of 100 possible core values. Please put a check mark next to your top 25 values, then circle your top 12 values, and put a star by your top 6. These are your core values.

Accountability	Decisiveness	Humility	Purpose
Achievement	Deliberate	Improvement	Quality
Adventure	Development	Independence	Reliability
Adversity	Diplomacy	Individualism	Reputation
Aesthetics	Diversity	Innovation	Resilience
Alignment	Education	Integrity	Respect
Ambition	Effectiveness	Intelligence	Responsibility
Analysis	Efficiency	Joy	Responsiveness
Authenticity	Empowerment	Judgment	Risk-taking
Authority	Ethical Practice	Justice	Safety
Balance	Fairness	Leadership	Security
Belonging	Faith	Logic	Self-acceptance
Change	Family	Love	Self-awareness
Challenge	Fitness	Loyalty	Self-discipline
Character	Forgiveness	Meaning	Self-esteem
Commitment	Freedom	Mindfulness	Spirituality
Community	Friendship	Moderation	Success
Compassion	Goal Setting	Morality	Teamwork
Competence	Happiness	Passion	Tolerance
Competition	Hard Work	Peace	Trust
Control	Harmony	Perfection	Truth
Cooperation	Health	Persistence	Urgency
Cost Control	Helping Others	Power	Wealth
Courage	Honesty	Preparation	Winning
Creativity	Honor	Productivity	Wisdom

Top 6 Core Values

1. _____
2. _____
3. _____
4. _____
5. _____
6. _____

WHAT MAKES YOUR HEART SING?

There are many different aspects of self-awareness, and they don't all involve psychological assessments or even values. Another way to better understand what makes you tick is just to ask yourself, "What makes my heart sing?"

No one can define for you what makes your heart sing. It might be sitting at the kitchen table on a Sunday morning making your to-do list, or playing a round of golf, or going to a movie. It can be anything. But it's important to think about what really makes you happy. Be aware of how different activities make you feel, then be open to recognizing this part of yourself. These pursuits, hobbies, or experiences may have nothing to do with your behaviors, your values, your personality type, or your skills, and that's fine. Finding joy is a personal thing.

Once you know what makes your heart sing, do more of it. Set aside time from work, family, and other responsibilities to do those things that bring you irrational pleasure. Life goes by faster than you think, so be sure to take time for things that naturally bring you personal joy and happiness.

CREATING YOUR PERSONAL INVENTORY

When I was about to graduate with my MBA from the University of North Carolina in 1973, I was excited and a bit anxious about my career, and I was about to step out on my own. I knew life was about to change, and I wanted to feel like I had some control over how it played out. So with a scratch pad and pencil, I made a list I called my personal inventory. The task, which I got from Gerry Bell, was to put down on one page all the important information I knew about myself, with the idea that these things should guide my life and career.

After finishing this inventory, I had a simple and clear understanding of myself, and was able to confidently navigate my early career and personal life.

A lot of people live their lives without really knowing who they are. What they think is self-knowledge may actually be a case of them doing what they think is expected of them or what others have told them they're good at. They wind up pursuing careers and chasing goals that don't align with their intrinsic values or natural strengths.

That all-too-common mistake is what this chapter has been trying to help you avoid. If you use the tools I've presented here and then really tap into the self-awareness that you gain, you will discover it's much easier to find success *and* happiness.

EXERCISE 4: PERSONAL INVENTORY

What do I like?

- _____
- _____
- _____
- _____
- _____

What do I not like?

- _____
- _____
- _____
- _____
- _____

What am I good at?

- _____
- _____
- _____
- _____
- _____

What am I not good at?

- _____
- _____
- _____
- _____
- _____

What are my natural talents?

- _____
- _____
- _____
- _____
- _____

What are my biggest weaknesses?

- _____
- _____
- _____
- _____
- _____

What are my motivating values?

- _____
- _____
- _____
- _____
- _____

What are my core values?

- _____
- _____
- _____
- _____
- _____

What is my life dream?

- _____
- _____
- _____
- _____
- _____

What makes my heart sing?

- _____
- _____
- _____
- _____
- _____

Chapter 10

THE GOODNESS OF HELPING OTHERS

"Each of us will one day be judged by our standard of
life, not by our standard of living; by our measure of
giving, not by our measure of wealth; by our simple
goodness, not by our seeming greatness."

—William Arthur Ward

We've spent a lot of time in the preceding chapters examining how to set and reach personal and professional goals. We've talked about the importance of looking deep inside yourself to discover exactly what you want out of life. But success doesn't happen in a vacuum. We can hardly do anything worthwhile in life without serving other people.

An unexamined life is not the only one that's not worth living. So is a life focused on just yourself. Consider how shocked Ebenezer Scrooge was when the Ghost of Christmas Future showed him the way people felt about him after his death. No one cared that he had piles of money—they remembered only that he was a selfish skinflint.

What a stark contrast with the atmosphere at the funeral for my good friend Bob Sapanaro. Bob, who died at sixty-five of pancreatic cancer, had a forty-year career with New York Life Insurance and was by any measure a successful businessman. But that's not what people in the large crowd at this funeral (well over 200 people) were talking about. Many of his closest friends eulogized him, telling funny stories that highlighted his humanity, not his career accomplishments. They remembered Bob had a gregarious personality, that he was a good family man and a true friend. The celebration of his life was about the joy and goodness he brought to his family and others.

That's what other people really care about—not your success, not your brilliance, and certainly not your wealth. They care about how you treat them. They care about how you make them feel. They care about your goodness.

As businesswoman Mary Kay Ash once said, "Everyone has an invisible sign hanging from their neck saying, 'Make me feel important.' Never forget this message when working with people." Think about how good it feels when you deal with someone who really listens and makes you feel like you matter. Whether it's your boss, your car mechanic, or your waitress, it gives you a real lift when someone is friendly and helpful. We're naturally grateful for the extra effort, and we think kindly of that person. So we should do everything we can to be that person for others.

We can trace the roots of goodness as far back as the beginning of Christianity and Jesus' call to "Love thy neighbor as thyself." From that point forward, our religion and our culture made it clear that how we treat others matters. In fact, we should treat them as well as we treat ourselves. And that's a high standard.

Nothing brings a deeper sense of fulfillment than helping others. Ironically, the best thing you can do for yourself is to do something for others. And if you doubt that, ask yourself what makes you feel better on Christmas morning: opening gifts from others or watching them open gifts from you?

Or if you're a parent, consider what you want for your children. Years ago, one of my favorite contemporary writers, Dennis Prager, gave a talk about raising children. He began by suggesting that parents identify what they most want their children to become, offering the following choices:

- Smart
- Successful
- Wealthy
- Happy
- Talented
- Good

As a father, I want our three sons to become all of these, and they are well on their way. But if I had to pick only one, it would be "good." And by good, I mean kind, decent, considerate, humble, caring, empathetic, honest, and all the other moral character traits mentioned in chapter 6. At the bottom of our hearts, I think this is really what all parents want most for their children.

As human beings, we can never flourish by just focusing on ourselves. Helping others leads to a richer, deeper, and more meaningful life. Being generous and considerate with others also leads to more self-esteem, and more personal success and happiness.

HELPING OTHERS IS AN AMERICAN TRADITION

"One of life's most important questions is—what am I doing for others?"

—Unknown

In the 1830s, French sociologist Alexis de Tocqueville came to the United States to study our prison system. He traveled around our growing country for almost a year while visiting our penitentiaries; then he returned to France to write his report.

In his travels, Tocqueville learned a lot about America and its people and how their culture differed from that of France and Western Europe. In 1835, he published the first of a two-volume work, *Democracy in America*, which interpreted American culture through the keen eyes of a thoughtful and well-read foreigner.

Tocqueville was especially impressed with how the early Americans helped each other. There was a real volunteer spirit that began with the pilgrims and then spread west. Because times were tough, people relied on their friends, their neighbors, and their communities for support. Indeed, their very survival depended on the help they received from each other.

This spirit of volunteerism continued to grow along with the country itself, developing into a mutually beneficial pattern as people took responsibility for solving their community's problems, first through collective efforts and later with private philanthropy. In Europe, Tocqueville noted, people tended to rely on government for these things, but Americans were different.

That spirit may not seem as alive today, but it's much stronger than you may think. In 2017, Americans gave $410 billion in philanthropy with another $193 billion worth of volunteer time donated by sixty-three million individuals. On a per-capita basis, American giving dwarfs the rate of giving in all other countries by a multiple of at least ten times. Helping others is clearly a big part of our American culture and the American DNA. We are a generous and community-minded people.

HELPING OTHERS HELPS YOU SUCCEED

"In business and in life, our rewards are directly related to how we serve others."

—Unknown

I didn't know it at the time, but my success as a homebuilder began in Dayton, Ohio, where I learned some valuable lessons in what *not* to do. My employer, Ryan Homes, and my boss and mentor, Don Howells, focused mainly on sales growth and the number of homes sold, and I saw firsthand the damage this strategy inflicted on our employees and our customers.

Ryan only had goals for sales and construction schedules, not quality or customer satisfaction. But because I witnessed the hassle and heartache a poorly built home created for our customers, I knew I wanted to do things differently when I started T.W. Lewis Company several years later.

SOLID GROUND

My mission to take the "hassle out of homebuilding" was no empty slogan; it was personal.

My view was that buyers deserved a well-built home and a hassle-free home-buying experience, and that should be included in every purchase. Our commitment to customer satisfaction was not a marketing program, and we weren't doing this to increase sales or profits. We did it because it was the right thing to do, and that led to a 95 percent satisfaction rate. But there it stuck because we weren't asking the customers what *they* wanted.

This insight was key. In homebuilding, there is something known as the "final walk." The customer walks through the home with the construction superintendent, looks it over, and creates a punch list of last-minute changes or fixes the company needs to make. Well, we began inviting our customers to come out a week before the final walk-through for what amounted to a pre-walk-through. They'd go through the house and tell us what they wanted done differently. We'd listen and then set about tweaking this and tweaking that. They'd come back a week later for the final walk-through and see we had honored their requests, and our customers loved it! To this day, I still hear from people thanking me for the quality we put into their homes.

Our customer satisfaction ratings edged up into the stratosphere, reaching a previously unheard of 98 percent. We were at the very top of our industry—because we had *listened*. As a byproduct of that, demand for our homes went up, and so did our prices and our profits. But that's not why we did it.

This cause-and-effect relationship between benefiting others and benefiting yourself is not an accident. If you look at famous entrepreneurs in history, from Henry Ford and Andrew Carnegie to Bill Gates and Steve Jobs, their enormous wealth was the direct result of the huge value their products added to the lives of their customers. The more value you provide to your customers, the more you benefit yourself.

This concept applies not only to business but also to life. In his book *Give and Take: Why Helping Others Drives Our Success* (2013), Wharton psychology professor Adam Grant describes his extensive research into three types of people:

- Givers. Those who strive to be generous with their time, energy, knowledge, skills, ideas, and connections. Their goal is to benefit others.

- Takers. Those who help others strategically so that the personal benefits exceed the personal costs. They seek personal gain.

- Matchers. Those who strive for an equal balance of personal benefits and costs. They seek fairness and tit for tat. No more, no less.

Grant's overall conclusion, with which I agree, is that we are all givers, takers, and matchers at different times and in different roles. But the longest lasting and most meaningful benefits will always accrue to the giver.

THE 60/40 PRINCIPLE

"People don't care about how much you know until they know how much you care."

—Theodore Roosevelt

When our oldest son, Tommy, turned thirteen in 1994, I began to experience the challenges that parents have with teenagers. When kids turn thirteen, the "teenage fairy" sucks their brains out (or so it seems to their parents). Their boundaries change rapidly, often without warning. They challenge curfews and other established rules daily, and parents become the least cool people on the planet.

Tommy was a great kid in every respect (and has since become a great young man), but the years from thirteen to eighteen were not easy. On his fifteenth birthday, he was supposed to be home at 9 p.m. but walked in the front door an hour late. I met him at the door and wasn't happy. And then he said something I will never forget: "Dad, I'm a man, and you treat me like a boy. And things have got to change!"

Rather than getting mad, I decided we needed to sit down for a long father-son talk. After each of us explained our reasoning and positions, I told him I would meet him more than halfway. I knew he was a good kid, and I was just being a protective father. When I told him I would move 60 percent in his favor if he would move 40 percent in mine, I could immediately see a sign of welcomed agreement in his eyes. That 60/40 principle became the new standard of our relationship through the rest of his teenage years and put us back on track with mutual love, respect, and trust.

This works with other people as well, not just with fathers and sons. By making it clear you are willing to go more than halfway with another person, you are showing that your relationship matters. You are demonstrating that you're a "giver." It takes courage to be the first one to take this step, but when others see this, human nature causes them to want to reciprocate. It's a win-win formula for improving any personal relationship.

HELPING OTHERS IMPROVES YOUR SELF-ESTEEM

"One of the kindest things that you can do for yourself is to help others."

—Unknown

One of my fondest memories of being a father is coaching our three sons in youth sports. Because my father had done this with me in Little League baseball and football, I always looked forward to doing the same for our boys. When Tommy turned five, I began my three-sport coaching career with baseball. A year later, we started basketball, and by the time Tommy was ten, we started flag football.

Each of these coaching experiences included about twelve to fifteen kids and lasted about three months, usually with practices on Saturday mornings and one or two games per week. It was a lot of fun but also required a lot of time and effort. It was worth it, however. I wasn't just sharing my love of sports with my sons and their friends. I was teaching the life lessons that come with playing sports—like the importance of hard work, discipline, teamwork, and winning and losing with grace. So for about ten years, most of my Saturday mornings and at least two nights per week were filled with coaching.

I was surprised by how seldom I saw the other fathers at practice or even at games. I couldn't understand what could possibly be more important than supporting your ten-year-old child at a Little League game.

These absent parents were certainly missing out. Going this extra mile for the boys certainly helped them, but by trying to help them, it unexpectedly helped me and actually increased my self-esteem. You can't build self-esteem from reading books or getting unearned praise. Kids may get "participation trophies" in school, but in real life, true self-esteem comes only from doing things that are estimable.

Think of someone you really admire and respect, and then ask the question, "Why do I admire and respect them?" My guess is that they have these estimable attributes:

- They are trustworthy, and do what they say they will do.
- They do the right thing, not the convenient thing.
- They are willing to invest their time and energy to help others.

Self-esteem is simply the level of respect and admiration you have for yourself. And if you want to boost self-esteem, there are no shortcuts. Doing more estimable things is the only way of increasing your self-respect and self-esteem.

THE PLATINUM RULE

"Mankind's greatest need is better understanding of man. All are victims of circumstance, all are under sentence of death, and all deserve pity."

—T.G. Lewis

Several years ago, a friend of mine in Phoenix wanted to help the homeless, but he didn't think he understood them well enough. He knew he couldn't get this knowledge from books or the Internet. So he decided to meet the homeless on their terms and on their turf. He disguised himself as a homeless person and walked the streets in Phoenix where they tended to hang out from midnight until the wee morning hours. He would sit down with homeless people and try to get to know them, learn their stories, understand their perspectives, and find out what their needs really were.

He discovered many of these people didn't just want a check or a handout. They didn't need our pity. They wanted dignity. They wanted to be recognized as human beings, and as children of God. If you're trying to help somebody, you need to know who they are. And you must remember that others are not just like you.

In taking this approach, my friend practiced the Platinum Rule, which is "Do unto others as they would like done unto themselves." Treating other people the way we want to be treated is certainly a step in the right direction, but it can cause us to fall short. Because we are all unique, we may wrongly assume that we know what others want or that they are just like us. But when we take the time to listen to others and to understand them, we begin to learn what they really need and how we can best help them. Treating others the way *they* want to be treated is the better way.

HELPING OTHERS INCREASES YOUR HAPPINESS

"Be willing to offer others the benefit of the doubt. Perhaps life simply gave them tougher problems than they could solve."

—Unknown

One of my favorite pleasures is being out in the woods and watching wildlife. Not only are the animals beautiful and graceful, they are also wild and free as they follow their instincts, without any inhibitions. Probably the most consistent and strongest instincts I've observed are how they protect their young and how they tend to live in groups. Sometimes they get separated, but they always regroup.

Human beings are like that. We need other people to be happy, and we derive natural pleasure and value from being part of a group. These groups begin with families and extend to clubs, schools, churches, teams, or the larger community—just as Alexis de Tocqueville observed in his travels through America almost 200 years ago. Engaging in the practice of giving and taking within groups of people gives us a sense of belonging, usefulness, and purpose—the foundation for happiness.

In today's Internet-based world, however, we often neglect this need. We sit at home with countless digital distractions and experience a pseudo-connectedness that gives us the illusion of togetherness. But when we see the rancor and spite that has come to dominate the tone of our national conversations, it quickly becomes apparent how deficient this modern community really is. The less we talk to real human beings face-to-face, the easier it is to settle into warring camps, which makes it harder than ever to practice selflessness.

As a young boy, I remember my mother often saying, "If you're feeling blue, lose five pounds and go to church." What she meant was, "To be happier, take some positive actions that will make you feel better about yourself." Helping others is one of the most positive actions we can take.

In chapter 20, "Understand Happiness," I list twenty different actions you can take to increase your personal happiness. But rest assured, the happiness mindset begins with changing your focus from yourself to others.

PART III

REACHING YOUR POTENTIAL

The Achiever's Model

Chapter 11

FIND YOUR TALENT

"The person born with a talent they are meant to use
will find their greatest happiness in using it."

—Johann Wolfgang von Goethe

Malcolm Gladwell was right. In his book *Outliers: The Story of Success*, he made a compelling argument for his theory that success is the result of talent, hard work, and good fortune. He supported his claims with specific examples, including Bill Gates, the Beatles, and even Canadian hockey players. As I interpreted it, his hard work was the 10,000 hours you had to put in early, and the good fortune was about good timing or special access to training and learning. But what did Gladwell mean by talent? What is talent really all about, how do we define it, and how does someone find it?

WHAT IS TALENT?

According to Bill Bonnstetter, who studied talent for over forty years and who created one of the world's largest assessment and training companies, talent includes seven different dimensions:

- Behaviors
- Motivators
- Personal Skills
- Acumen
- Emotional Intelligence
- Education
- Experience

Each of these seven dimensions is complex in itself, but when you expand talent to include all seven of them, the complexity increases, and you can begin to understand how difficult it is to find and develop your talent. Simply put, this complexity explains why starting early and staying late is so important to success. It takes a lot of time and hard work to realize your talents. But let's take a deeper look at these seven dimensions from a practical standpoint:

- Behaviors. I talk about these in chapter 9. They are largely hard-wired, so becoming aware of them and understanding them will help you improve your natural strengths.

- Motivators. I also cover these in chapter 9. These are fairly stable but can shift over time. You will need to stay aligned with your primary motivating values to best find your talents.

- Personal Skills. These include the twenty-three skills referenced in the Indigo Report. Each one is a talent to be used. Your top five are your natural talents, and you need to use them often to help you succeed. It is also important to carefully choose your role models and learn from their skills and habits.

- Acumen. Acumen is the natural ability to understand other people, systems, and yourself to make better decisions. This improves with experience. The more experiences, the better.

- Emotional Intelligence. This skill involves perceiving, understanding, and managing emotions and feelings. This also improves with effort and experience. The more effort and experience, the more earned confidence, the more emotional intelligence will grow.

- Education. This is one dimension where you are largely in control. You must do a lot of learning, in and out of the classroom, so taking responsibility for it makes a big difference in developing your talent.

- Experience. This is the "dot" that Steve Jobs discussed when he connected a college class on calligraphy to the design of the Apple computer. The more experiences you have, the more energy you invest in your work. The more lessons you learn from those experiences, the more you nurture your talent.

In every person there is a seed of greatness. Understanding your uniqueness, your values, your natural strengths, and your authenticity is vital to finding your success.

IS TALENT OVERRATED?

"Hard work beats talent if talent doesn't work hard."

—Sign in the University of Kentucky football weight room

The answer to this question is yes, and no. In his book *Talent Is Overrated: What Really Separates World-Class Performers from Everybody Else* (2010), Geoff Colvin explores the mystery of high performance. To summarize some of the book's more perceptive reviewers, "High performance is not just the result of hard work or natural talent, or even the combination of both." What really makes all the difference is hard work combined with natural talent, *plus* what Colvin terms "deliberate practice."

What is deliberate practice? It isn't the kind of hard work your parents told you about. It's harder. It's more difficult. It hurts. It takes discipline. It requires a regimen. It takes the drive to continually challenge yourself. But most encouragingly, the superior performance resulting from deliberate practice isn't reserved for a special few. The price may be high—but it is available to us all.

Because deliberate practice takes discipline, regimen, and energy, it creates adversity. Overcoming this adversity on a regular basis builds resilience. There is much talk today about how to create resilience, but you can't really teach it or create it in others, and you can't get it from reading a book. Resilience comes from overcoming an obstacle or a setback, which builds the confidence you need to overcome the next one. When deliberate practice becomes a habit, resilience becomes part of your personal character, and your talent increases. The cycle goes like this:

Hard Work/Talent Cycle

BUILDING RESILIENCE

"Don't let anyone stop you. There will be times when you'll be disappointed, but you can't stop. Make yourself the very best that you can make out of what you are. The very best."

—Sadie Alexander

Think of resilience as a muscle. To be strong, you must use and challenge your muscles. When you take on difficult assignments or challenges, you usually find them hard, and you may initially fail or get knocked down. When you get knocked down, you use your resilience muscle to get back up. When you get into the habit of pushing yourself, getting knocked down and getting back up often, you build a strong resilience muscle, preparing yourself for the next inevitable challenge you will encounter on the road to success.

You can only build resilience through experience. You don't get it from watching others, going to classes, or reading books. So even if you haven't had the best role models in your life, you can still develop your resilience muscle by challenging yourself and pushing through the inevitable adversity that follows.

EMBRACING ADVERSITY

"Adversity is like a strong wind. It tears away from us all but the things that cannot be torn, so that we see ourselves as we really are."

—Arthur Golden

Finding your talent is not easy because it requires you to overcome adversity. The more you take on difficult challenges, the more your talent will improve. For me, the least enjoyable years of my life were the three years I spent in Dayton, Ohio, where I experienced "homebuilder boot camp" but came away with the knowledge and confidence it took to succeed in this industry. I could have easily avoided this unpleasant experience and taken another job in a nicer city, closer to my friends and family. I would have had a lot more fun in my twenties, but I didn't choose the path of least resistance. In hindsight, it was one of the best career decisions I ever made.

I later learned from reading Meg Jay's *The Defining Decade* (2012) that your twenties really are the decade where you can best build your root structure, complete your education, push yourself, and encounter some adversity to begin to find your talent.

When I was having such a miserable time in Dayton, I never thought about quitting. Not even once. I was sick with hay fever half the time, the people I worked with made my daily life hard, but I had a clear goal—to be promoted to division manager—and I was not going to let anything deter me. And my talent improved.

WHAT ARE YOU NATURALLY GOOD AT?

"Don't worry about your passion; that changes over time. Find your talent—what you're naturally good at—and work on that. It's your best chance of making a difference in this world."

—T.W. Lewis

To find your talent, one of the best questions to ask yourself is, "What am I naturally good at, with little or no effort?" Another good question is, "What do I do so well that other people would be happy to pay me to do it for them?" You can generate a short list of things that come to mind and then ask your best friends, your boss, and your parents—much as I did with my personal inventory at Chapel Hill. Sometimes other people can see your talent better than you can. Whatever you conclude from this exercise is probably a good indication of your talent. It's what you're naturally good at. But then you need to develop it with hard work and deliberate practice, which will create adversity and build your resilience.

One of the most important "dots" I have connected over the years is how much of my behavior and success is rooted in my hardwired motivating values and behavioral traits. My strong utilitarian and individualist motivating values were perfectly aligned with being an entrepreneur and running a real estate development and homebuilding business. And my high dominance and fast-paced behavioral styles were well-suited to the construction industry. Because these values and behaviors were natural to me, work seemed like fun, so I worked a lot. And the more I worked, the more my talents developed.

You'll find your talents in your natural strengths, motivators, behaviors, and skills, so the sooner you know and understand them, the better! It is much easier to improve a natural strength than to try to improve a weakness. And your time will be better spent.

FOLLOW YOUR PASSION OR YOUR TALENT?

"Everyone has talent at twenty-five. The difficulty is to have it at fifty."

—Edgar Degas

As a high school and college student, my passion was mainly sports, especially football and basketball. And it still is! But I wasn't big enough or fast enough to compete beyond high school sports. Had I pursued this passion after college, I would have surely had little success.

But because I never really got enough sports as a young man, I have had a tremendous amount of fun and joy my entire life being an avid sports fan. Passions that don't include much natural talent can still be great hobbies to enjoy, but when it comes to reaching your career potential, following your talent is a much better plan.

You will always have time outside of work, so that's the place to pursue those passions. Don't give up on them—but if you have A-level talent in one field and B-minus talent in another, make the first one your career and the second one your hobby.

FINDING YOUR TALENT IN TWO WORDS

"It's easy to make it hard, and it's hard to make it easy."

—Unknown

During my 400-plus scholarship interviews with high school seniors, I always asked them, "So what do you want to do when you grow up?" They would usually say something like, "I love computers and travel, so I want to be an international computer consultant" or "I am good at statistics and love biology, so I want to be a statistical biologist."

There were usually two keywords that came out of their mouths that combined their passions and their talents. When I was a senior in college, my two words were "construction" and "investment." I just became energized every time I heard those two words, and I still do! I built my entire career around those two words because they excited me, inspired me, and aligned with my motivating values. Because the construction and investment industries resonated with me, I didn't mind putting in the long hours, and my talents kept getting better.

When you find your talent, you've found your sweet spot. There are few things sadder than older men and women who didn't cultivate their talents and in middle age are filled with regret over things they didn't do. You don't want to be fifty years old and stuck in a boring job that doesn't challenge you or make good use of your talents.

What are your two words? I believe your answer to this question will point you in the right direction.

Chapter 12

MAKE GOOD DECISIONS

"When it comes to being successful in life, having good judgment and making good decisions are far more important than just being smart."

—T.W. Lewis

As a young boy of thirteen or fourteen years of age, I began to notice how some of my friends were different from others. The ones who always went to class, did their homework, and got involved in sports and other school activities seemed to do pretty well. Take David Monthie, for example, a friend of mine who was our class valedictorian. David was a serious student—smart, disciplined, and engaged with high school clubs and activities. He later received a scholarship to Yale University and went on to become a successful lawyer.

Then there was the boy I'll call Joe Johnson. Joe and I were good friends in the eighth and ninth grades at Bryan Station Junior High. Joe, too, was a smart kid and a talented basketball player. He was also from a broken home, had no father, and loved to gamble, even in the eighth grade! I'll never forget sitting under a tree with him after school one day when he said, "See those two birds on the telephone line over there? I bet you a dollar the one on the left flies first."

If you'll bet on that, you'll take a chance on anything. Joe took a lot of unnecessary risks. He would break into the high school gym on weekends to shoot hoops. He began to hang out with the wrong people and quit playing sports. As he continued to make more bad decisions, things kept getting worse for him. The last I heard from Joe, he was divorced, broke, and about to be evicted from his home—the predictable result of a lifetime of bad decisions.

Then I thought about my grandfather, Daddy Buck. Daddy Buck made very solid personal and professional decisions. He didn't drink alcohol (except for an occasional sip), was always busy and industrious, was very involved with his community and his church, loved his job working for the L&N Railroad for fifty years, and was clearly dedicated to his family. He was also cheerful, had lots of friends, and his home was always a happy and peaceful place. His life reflected the good decisions he had made.

With my dad, I could see how things were very different. Daddy was also a smart and talented man, but he was not a good decision maker. After he retired from the navy when I was twelve, he no longer had the military structure to keep him in line, and I watched how his poor decisions caused his life to unravel. From this experience, I learned early that your decisions really matter, and they not only impact you but also everyone around you.

No one is perfect. We all make some bad decisions. But while you can recover from a bad business decision, which is measured in dollars, bad personal decisions are often much more expensive and harder to overcome. Choices like criminal behavior, bad marriages, gambling, or abuse of drugs or alcohol can ruin your life.

Becoming a good decision maker is highly underrated as a requirement for success. Any person who regularly makes good decisions will be successful. Although the future is uncertain, there are several simple models you can follow to improve your decision-making skills. Knowing your goals and values makes good decision making much easier.

SOLID GROUND

MAKING DECISIONS UNDER UNCERTAINTY

"Life can be hard. And if you make bad decisions, it can be really hard!"

—Unknown

One of my favorite scholarship interview questions is "What do you think are the two most important decisions you'll ever make?" Most high school seniors stumbled a bit on this at first but usually concluded that they were 1) who they marry and 2) the career they choose. I would agree with this, and then I asked, "How many people get both of these right?" We all know that about 50 percent of marriages end in divorce, and my guess is that less than half of all workers choose the right career for themselves. This means that about one in four people gets both of these decisions right, and each of these decisions has huge implications for personal success and happiness. So how can you avoid making life-altering bad decisions?

All your decisions involve the future, which is uncertain, so you need to be prepared to mitigate or manage these risks when making daily decisions. Some of these decisions are small, like what clothes to wear, and others are more important, like how to prepare for your next meeting. Some are really big, like who you should marry or whether you should take a new job or keep your current one. All decisions involve evaluating your options, then using your judgment to make the best decision possible so that you can achieve your goals. It is almost impossible to make good decisions if you don't have clarity on your goals, priorities, and values.

As Yogi Berra once said, "It's tough to make predictions, especially about the future!" But there are ways to factor in this uncertainty and make good decisions in spite of it. Let's review some of the best decision-making models I've learned over the years.

143

SEVEN STEPS

"I am not a product of my circumstances. I am a product of my decisions."

—Stephen Covey

Ideally, there are seven basic steps to take before making every decision:

1. Clarify your goals and values. What are the outcomes you want to achieve with this decision?

2. Do your research. What are the facts? What is subjective? What else do you need to know so that you really understand the issue? (This step is especially important for big decisions.)

3. Examine your alternatives. You can't make a decision until you clarify your choices.

4. Evaluate each of your alternatives against your goals and your values. This will make the best decision much easier to find.

5. Make a decision. Choose the alternative that best fits your goals and values.

6. Sleep on it. Once you've made an important decision, think about it, and make sure you are committed to it. If you're not, delay your decision.

7. Commit and take action. Now you are on the way to achieving your goal, and your confidence will increase.

Obviously, we can't formally go through all seven of these steps for every decision, and there is no need to do so for minor decisions, but understanding the process of making a good decision will help you improve your decision-making skills.

KNOW YOUR VALUES

"It's easy to make good decisions when you know your values."

—T.W. Lewis

When Jan and I were raising our three sons, times were usually pretty hectic, and we had way more things to do than we had time to do them. With children, marriage, a demanding job, and other responsibilities needing our attention, it became impossible to fit everything in. So I had to make some hard choices. As I mentioned earlier, my top three priorities were family, career, and health, and there was no way I was going to sacrifice my commitment to any of them. Getting clear on this made it much easier to say no to less important things.

Once you have clarified your goals and your core values, making good decisions gets much easier. Look at your options and ask yourself, "What best aligns with my values?" Choosing this option is almost always the best decision and is a great habit to help you live consistently within your values. This will also increase your happiness and reduce the possibility of doing something you will later regret.

TWO TIMES TO DECIDE

"There are only two times to make a decision: when you have all the information, and when you have to."

—Unknown

As the CEO of a homebuilding company for twenty-five years, almost every day I would have an employee or a customer ask me to make a quick decision. Sometimes the answer was clear and urgent enough that I would decide immediately. But usually, I would say, "Let me get back to you on this." Then I would gather more information, think about it, and come to a more thoughtful and better decision. When time allows, no decision is usually the best decision you can make.

Many people make important decisions before they really have to and end up getting themselves into trouble. The message here is to delay important decisions for as long as you can and use this extra time to continue to do more research and gather more information so you are better prepared to make the best decision possible.

THINK. RETHINK.

"Fate is the hand of cards we've been dealt.
Choice is how we play the hand."

—Marshall Goldsmith

When it comes to critical thinking, one of the best ways to make a really big decision is to sit down and first go through the seven-step decision-making process. Write down your goals, your values, look at all your possible choices, and come to a complete, *preliminary* decision. Then put it away for a few days, get more input from others, and do more research.

Whenever possible, sleep on it. Give it time. Come back to the question with a fresh perspective. The additional information or insights gained even within a few days can lead you to a better decision.

Sometimes, when we are stuck on a complex problem or decision, we just need to talk it out with others whose judgment we respect. In these cases, I recommend picking three different people with three different outlooks, and talking it over with them. Then take good notes on the advice of each and compare them. Where do they overlap? Where do they diverge? What new considerations did they identify?

With fresh thinking from others, along with some of your own, you're in a position to re-evaluate your preliminary decision and make sure you're considering all the important factors and perspectives. Then you can re-think the previous decision, improve it, and confidently move forward. Rethinking is a great way to make better decisions.

And remember that Bob Dylan song; everyone wants you to be just like them. So take the advice with a grain of salt. Consider the opinions of others, but make up your own mind based on your goals and your values.

MODERATION AND THE GOLDEN MEAN

"Moderation is the golden mean between two extremes."

—Aristotle

I often find myself faced with a decision between two very different choices, where I'm not really comfortable with either. In these cases, I try to find the middle ground—the moderate approach. It can be as simple as taking a step in someone else's direction, like the 60/40 approach I mentioned earlier, or some kind of negotiated compromise that leaves both parties satisfied.

As I have gained more life experience, I have learned to see the wisdom in moderation. When you apply the principle of moderation to decision making, you get compromise. As long as the compromise doesn't violate important values or principles, finding and choosing the common ground is usually the best decision you can make. In the long run, mutually satisfactory outcomes are always better, because they help to maintain strong personal relationships.

TWO TYPES OF BAD DECISIONS

When Jan and I were raising our three young sons, we heard of a simple child-raising technique called "refrigerator rules," which meant having no more than five simple rules of behavior, which we stuck to the refrigerator door so everyone would see them often. Our five refrigerator rules were as follows:

1. Do what Mom and Dad say the first time; no back talk.
2. No hitting, no hurting.
3. Make a mess, clean it up.
4. Break it, fix it.
5. Don't do anything stupid.

Rule number five became our whole family's favorite because it covered everything and called for good judgment. To this day, with all three sons fully grown, we still say, "Don't forget rule number five."

What we were really trying to teach them was not to make bad decisions. But bad decisions can come in two forms:

- Type 1—Doing something stupid.
- Type 2—Not doing something smart.

Type 1 bad decisions are pretty easy to identify. They get you in trouble. Avoiding Type 1 bad decisions is a form of playing defense. It stops you from losing, but it doesn't make you win. Type 2 bad decisions, which are much more subtle, can be just as harmful in the long run. They keep you from moving toward your goal. None of us wants to do anything stupid, but we should be mindful of some of the smarter things we *could* be doing, because avoiding Type 2 bad decisions is just as important.

JUDGMENT

"A decision is the action a person must take when he has information so incomplete that the answer does not suggest itself."

—Arthur W. Radford

In 1802, Thomas Jefferson made a gutsy decision to acquire the Louisiana Purchase from Napoleon of France. But this decision to buy 530 million acres for $15 million (approximately three cents per acre) led to severe criticism by many experts of that era. Some said, "We are buying land we don't need with money we don't have!" This argument may have sounded good, but it missed the point.

Jefferson was exercising his solid judgment. He believed the purchase was a terrific bargain because it would allow the United States to gain control of the Mississippi River and open the American West to further growth, leading to a great nation bounded by two major oceans. In hindsight, he was certainly right.

SOLID GROUND

Judgment is probably the most important and rarest of all the qualities it takes to make good decisions. Judgment begins with knowledge, grows with experience, matures with understanding truth, and then becomes wisdom—which is the ultimate best tool for good decision making. It goes like this:

- Knowledge + Experience + Truth = Wisdom
- Wisdom + Action = Judgment

Making good decisions is not a team sport; it's a personal responsibility. To make personal decisions with solid judgment, you just can't count on third parties, friends, experts, or popular opinions. You really have to count on yourself—your knowledge, your experiences, your values, and your judgment.

Once you learn the tools of decision making and have clarity on your goals and values, making good decisions will get easier, your life will get better, and your chances of success and happiness will improve. You can be sure of it.

Chapter 13

TAKE SMART RISKS

*"You will never reach new horizons if you are afraid to
lose sight of the shore."*

—Unknown

Several years ago, I gave a talk in Chapel Hill on entrepreneurship
to a group of undergraduate business students at the University of
North Carolina. I told them my story about starting my own company, stepping out on my own, taking on millions of dollars in personally
guaranteed debt, and staking my young family's future on the success of
my new company.

During the talk I explained that if you look up the word entrepreneur
in the dictionary, you will see that it is defined as "one who initiates and
takes risk." Then one student asked: "How did you justify taking the risk of
starting your own company?"

My answer was this: Through experience, I had become confident in
my ability to take and manage risks. I was less worried about having my
future in my own hands than I was about having it in the hands of someone else.

Jan and I had three children at home at the time, and while children
sometimes make people more risk-averse, I had developed the competence

150

and confidence that comes from a diverse set of experiences. And I knew I could succeed.

Not everyone is comfortable taking risks, but we all need to realize that risks are part of life and are unavoidable. If we try to play it too safe, we can be sure our rewards will be small. But if we can grow comfortable taking smart risks, and learn how to manage and mitigate them, the rewards will surely follow.

Risk and rewards go together. To get the rewards, we have to take the risks. Knowing how to take risks, when to take risks, and how to mitigate risks is essential to achieving success.

GETTING COMFORTABLE BEING UNCOMFORTABLE

"Security is mostly a superstition. It does not exist in nature."

—Helen Keller

Several years ago, our family took a photo safari trip to Botswana to see the beautiful African wildlife in their natural habitat. We visited three different camps over our ten-day vacation, and our favorite one, by far, was called Mombo. In Setswana, the language of Botswana, "Mombo" means plenty, and we soon learned just how fitting that word was.

At Mombo, we were in the Okavango Delta, so there was plenty of water, plenty of plants, plenty of prey, and plenty of predators. Nowhere had we seen such an obvious natural food chain. The water grew the plants, the plants attracted the birds and small game, and the small game attracted the big predators like hyenas, leopards, and lions.

There was constant change every day, and every species was on guard against the risks they faced. These risks were unavoidable, and the animals knew it. They knew they were potentially dinner for someone. So they used their natural strengths—speed, size, ability to climb—to protect themselves and survive. It was the real world, and they seemed comfortable being un-comfortable. But they were cautious and aware of their surroundings.

As human beings, we, too, feel instinctive motivation to seek safety and survival—so change, unpredictability, and volatility make us uncomfortable. But these are also the precise conditions that present opportunities if we are able to embrace the risks. After all, as Dwight Eisenhower supposedly said, "If you want total security, go to prison. There you're fed, clothed, given medical care, and so on. The only thing lacking…is freedom."

UNDERSTANDING UNCERTAINTY

"Twenty years from now you will be more disappointed by the things you didn't do than by the things you did."

—Mark Twain

One common definition of risk is the exposure to injury or loss. But this cautious definition (probably written by a low risk-taker) fails to include the *benefits* of taking risks, which include the exposure to success, achievement, joy, and meaning.

Think of risk-taking as the art of managing uncertainty to achieve a goal. We live in a world that is full of uncertainty, and as much as we want to feel like we are in control of everything, we need to understand the difference between certainty and uncertainty and use that understanding to our advantage.

Strangely, most popular books about success avoid the subject of risk, or they downplay it, as if being lucky is just as important as being a smart risk-taker. Maybe it's just that risk-takers don't write books. In any event, it's a critically important skill to possess in all walks of life. A good risk-taker knows what is controllable and what is uncertain (what you can't control).

Once you have a handle on all the uncertain things that might happen, you can then create a plan to deal with the worst-case scenarios. What's the worst that can happen if you take this risk and it doesn't work out?

If the worst-case scenario is that you are financially ruined, then it's not a risk worth taking. If, on the other hand, the worst-case scenario is that you suffer a tolerable loss but a gain is a much likelier outcome, well, then it might be a risk worth taking. After you've examined worst-case scenarios and accepted their likelihood, risk doesn't seem so scary. That's how to get comfortable being uncomfortable.

MEASURING RISK

"Be fearful when others are greedy, and be greedy when others are fearful."

—Warren Buffett

Warren Buffett's advice may sound like stubborn contrarianism, but in financial markets it is absolutely sound. When the stock market crashed in 2008, the most sophisticated investors doubled down and won big. And then the housing market in Phoenix crashed, and prices dropped more than 50 percent, but there were no retail buyers—even at a 50 percent discount. The market was gripped with fear. And what happened?

Shrewd local and national investors came in and quietly bought thousands of houses, some for as little as $30,000, and leased them to people who were afraid to *buy*. Five years later, these investors were able to sell these houses for big gains and were richly rewarded for their risk. Why did they think this would be a good investment, and how did they measure their risks? Let's review four proven business principles that will help you understand risk.

Profit Margin

I once had a good friend who owned a large chain of grocery stores. In the grocery business, profit margins are very low, typically in the 1 percent to 2 percent of revenue range. In other words, you have to sell $1 million worth of groceries to make a profit of $10,000 to $20,000, which makes for a high-cost, low-margin, high-risk business.

When Walmart and Amazon decided to get into the grocery business in Phoenix, my friend had to compete with them, and his narrow margin turned negative, forcing his business into bankruptcy. With margins so small, his business just had no room for any unexpected changes. The rewards no longer justified the risks.

Probably the easiest way to measure the risk of a business decision is to evaluate the profit margin that we expect to achieve versus the risk (exposure to loss) we might encounter. In the homebuilding business, before we would commit to buying land for a new project, we would calculate the realistic revenues and costs to determine the expected profit margin. Usually, this margin would be between 5 and 10 percent. The higher the expected profit margin, the lower the risk. Anything under 5 percent was out, and anything over 10 percent was a go. But if it was between 5 and 10 percent, we had to dig deeper into the details to see how we could get to an expected profit margin of 10 percent. If we could, we would move forward. If not, we would pass.

Margin of Safety

Before you buy into a risky venture, you really need to do your home-work to uncover everything that could go wrong. Once you have done this, you can be better prepared to understand and deal with any adversity that comes your way.

To understand the concept of margin of safety, ask yourself what you stand to lose and how much is safe. If you're playing blackjack in Las Vegas and put $100 on the table, you stand to lose it all, so your margin of safety is zero. If you are investing in a stock, your safety margin is probably in the 80 percent range and gets much better the longer you hold it.

When Phoenix home investors looked at the bet they were taking, they could see prices had already fallen well below replacement costs and couldn't fall much more. And if they did, it would probably be less than 20 percent, so their margin of safety was at least 80 percent. Because they could easily cover their holding costs by renting the homes until the market recovered, they could see this was a safe risk, and they capitalized on the opportunity.

Return on Investment

Probably the most basic way to look at risk is with the return on investment, or ROI principle. In financial markets, the expected returns are based on the perceived risks in each investment category. For example, the expected annual returns for five- to ten-year corporate bonds are now in the 4 to 5 percent range, while the expected annual returns for most stocks are in the 7 to 9 percent range, because they are more volatile. The point here is that your return must justify your risk. The bigger your risk, the bigger your expected return should be.

As a partner with Trammell Crow Residential in the 1980s, we had a very simple way of managing risk. We knew that if things went badly, we would lose 100 percent of our investment. So, to justify this risk, we tried to achieve a profit that was at least ten times our investment. This was a high mark that we rarely hit, but this discipline helped keep us out of trouble.

Volatility

The Sharpe ratio was developed in 1966 to address volatility (standard deviation) in the stock market as a risk that required investors to seek higher returns. The concept is that higher volatility (large swings in value) creates more risk that should be rewarded in the long run by higher returns. The more stable the investment, the lower the volatility, the lower the risk, and the lower the expected return.

The higher the Sharpe ratio, the more return investors should expect to receive in return for the extra volatility to which they are exposed. The Sharpe ratio message is clear: Change, uncertainty, and volatility all provide opportunities for taking smart risks that will achieve higher returns.

MITIGATING RISK

On another one of our trips to Africa, Jan and I were on safari with a young South African guide and his experienced tracker, who sat on the front of the vehicle to look for footprints and other signs of wildlife. Our guide told us this person was one of the best lion trackers in all of South Africa, so I watched him carefully.

When other guides walked out into the bush, I noticed they carried their rifles, but this tracker brought only his eyes, ears, and brain. When I asked him how he avoided danger, he said, "When I follow an animal's tracks, I keep my head up to look and listen for signs of danger, and I keep my head down because I don't want to find a foot in the track!" This lion tracker had just explained the key to managing risk—you pay attention to the big picture (head up) and the little picture (head down)! Let's review four ways I have learned to mitigate risks.

Fundamental Position

As a high school football player, one of the first things I learned was on defense you always had to be prepared for anything. We called this fundamental position, which we defined as follows:

- Both feet solidly on the ground at shoulder width.
- Both legs bent slightly, ready to spring into action in any direction.
- Both arms hanging straight down, hands just above the knees, ready to shed a block or make a tackle.
- Head up and eyes alert.

Fundamental position is another perfect model for managing risk. Like the lion tracker, be alert and ready for anything.

Diversification

"If you put all your eggs in one basket, you need to really watch that basket."

—Andrew Carnegie

Another popular risk-management tool, often applied to portfolio theory, is diversification. The theory here is that different asset classes (e.g., bonds, stocks, real estate, and energy, etc.) are not correlated and move in different directions at different times.

The principle of diversification is a good one and can be applied to every aspect of your life. By having more diversity, you are less dependent on any one thing, and your total portfolio is safer.

SOLID GROUND

Ripcord

"Risk and reward go together. If you want the rewards, you will have to take the risks."

—T.W. Lewis

In the world of business, the best risk managers have an exit plan for each major risk they take. At Amazon, one of the fastest growing companies in the world, they call it the double-swinging door. What they mean by this is that for every door they walk through (risks they take), they need the ability to turn around and exit. Amazon takes a lot of large risks, but they always have an exit plan to limit their losses if things go badly. Then they do their best to make it work.

At Trammell Crow Residential, we followed a similar strategy that we called the "ripcord." For every investment we made, we limited our liabilities and negotiated an exit strategy. If the deal went poorly, we made sure we had a ripcord (exit plan) that we could pull to minimize our losses and parachute to safety. The real estate developers who didn't practice this principle ended up being victims of the recession.

Alignment

One of the less-talked-about risk-management principles (which I didn't really learn until late in my career) is the power and safety of alignment. By alignment, I mean having your goals and values aligned with the people with whom you associate in your business and personal life.

In the homebuilding business, our values were clear—quality, customer service, and profits—so alignment with our trades was usually pretty good. But getting alignment in philanthropy and investing in new ventures gets a lot harder. I have learned you can take risks with markets or money but not with people that you don't trust. Dealing with people of integrity is always the first priority.

HUNTERS AND FARMERS

"A ship is safe in the harbor, but that is not what ships are made for."

—John A. Shedd

In the business world, it is pretty easy to see the differences in people when it comes to their orientation to risk. The real estate developers, entrepreneurs, and many financial executives are the risk-takers. The accountants, property managers, and many administrative people are the steady ones who are less inclined to take risks. They value their security and safety more. In the Trammell Crow days, we often spoke of the high risk-takers as the hunters and the low risk-takers as the farmers.

To understand your approach to risk-taking, it is helpful to look at your personal behaviors and motivating values as described in chapter 9 and assess your own orientation toward risk. When it comes to personal behaviors, I have learned that the following human differences are largely true:

- High Dominance people are more likely to be comfortable with risk than Low Dominance people.

- High Influencing people are more persuasive and assertive than Low Influencing people, so they are more comfortable being risk-takers than Low Influencers.

- High Steadiness people don't like change, so they are more likely to avoid risk than Low Steadiness people who like a fast, changing environment.

- High Compliance people value following the rules and covering all the details more than Low Compliance people, so they would likely be slower and more careful when it comes to risk.

Motivating values also have a big impact on an individual's approach to taking risks:

- High Theoreticals value knowledge more than action, so they tend to be low risk-takers.

- High Utilitarians value efficiency and economic rewards, so they will be comfortable taking risks when they are justified by the rewards.

- High Aesthetics value beauty and creativity, so they may be somewhat more prone to risk than Low Aesthetics if the risk helps them achieve their values.

- High Socials value helping people, so they will be willing to take risks if they are convinced it will help others.

- High Individualists value recognition and control, so they tend to be willing to take risks if they believe it will improve their image or reputation.

- High Traditionals value traditions, structure, and principles, so they may be slower to take risk than Low Traditionals.

In other words, your behaviors and motivating values have a big influence on your personal goals and on your level of comfort when it comes to taking risks. Being conscious of these biases will help you become a better risk-taker.

THE RISK OF NOT TAKING RISKS

"You miss 100 percent of the shots you don't take."

—Wayne Gretzky

Positive Coaching Alliance is a national nonprofit organization that works with thousands of coaches and young athletes to teach lessons of hard work, discipline, competition, toughness, and resilience. Its mission is to "create better athletes and better people," and its model for helping coaches and young athletes is simple. It's called the ELM Tree Model:

- E—Effort
- L—Learning
- M—Mistakes

The lesson here is, if you don't put forth the effort that exposes you to the risk of failing, you deny yourself the opportunity to learn from your mistakes. This model could also be expressed as follows:

- Wake up
- Work hard
- Take risks
- Make mistakes
- Learn
- Repeat

If you talk to anyone who has taken risks and succeeded in any area, they will tell you that each mistake or failure taught them valuable lessons. And if they had not been willing to take these risks, they never would have learned the lessons that led to their success.

COMPETENCE LEADS TO CONFIDENCE

"It is not the critic who counts, not the man who points out how the strong man stumbles or where the doer of deeds could have done them better. The credit belongs to the man who is actually in the arena, whose face is marred by dust and sweat and blood; who strives valiantly; who errs, who comes up short again and again ... who spends himself in a worthy cause; who at the best, knows in the end, the triumph of high achievement; and who at the worst, if he fails, at least fails while daring greatly."

—Theodore Roosevelt

When I took the biggest business risk of my life and started my own company, I had worked in five different cities for four different companies with six different bosses over eighteen years. I had made a lot of mistakes and learned a lot of lessons. From all this effort and experience, I had become competent in my field and was confident that I could make this business succeed. Without this competence and confidence, I would never have been able to take the risk that led to my business success.

You can't go through life without taking risks, so be the person who strives, who takes smart risks, and gives it your all. And when you lose, as you sometimes will, get right back up and into the arena. That's a life without regrets and a life worth living.

Chapter 14

KEEP YOUR DRIVE ALIVE

"Always bear in mind that your own resolution to succeed
is more important than any other one thing."

—Abraham Lincoln

*A*fter you commit to your own success, you will find many obstacles on the road to achievement. And it takes a lot of energy, persistence, resiliency, and ambition to overcome these obstacles. Sustaining these qualities over a long period of time is called drive.

Drive and ambition may seem like more or less the same thing, but they're not. Ambition is a desire for achievement. Drive is an action word; it is energy and movement. Ambition is good, but in a way, it is almost passive; drive is ambition with energy and action.

Yet some people in today's popular culture seem to discourage ambition and drive, as if these traits are too competitive or aggressive and encourage people to be "less equal." For instance, this is how my dictionary.com app used the word ambition in a sentence: "Too much ambition caused him to be disliked by his colleagues." Really?

Unfortunately, that's what many young people are learning in school. Don't stand out from the crowd. Herd up with the rest of the sheep. This subversive redefining of good solid words—morality, character, judgment, ambition—will have harmful effects on those who take them to heart. As the story of Abraham Lincoln shows us, drive and ambition are attributes of good character, and they make great things possible.

A RESOLUTION TO SUCCEED

Among his many other personal qualities, Abraham Lincoln embodied what we call drive. In his early years, he easily could have been considered one of the least likely candidates for success of any kind.

Born in a one-room log cabin on February 12, 1809, just south of Hodgenville, Kentucky, Lincoln's beginnings were humble. His parents lost their small farm in 1816, and moved to Spencer County, Indiana, where his mother, Nancy, took ill with "milk sickness" in 1818, and died. Young Abraham was only nine years old.

Within a year, Lincoln's father, Thomas, remarried a widow named Sara Bush Johnson. Abraham's new mother brought order to the Lincoln family's one-room cabin and taught Abraham how to spell and write. He quickly became a voracious reader and would walk miles to borrow a new book. In addition to the family's King James Bible, Lincoln read Parson Weems' *Life of Washington* (1809), William Grimshaw's *History of the United States* (1820), and John Bunyan's *Pilgrim's Progress* (1678). These books left lasting impressions on him.

In 1828, he hired on as a deckhand on a flatboat taking cargo down the Ohio and Mississippi rivers to New Orleans. After his return from the second trip in July 1831, he wound up going with the owner of the flatboat to a small town north of Springfield, Illinois, called New Salem. At age twenty-two, Lincoln was nothing more than a "piece of floating driftwood," as he later described himself.

But in New Salem, Abraham Lincoln found opportunities for self-improvement. He constantly borrowed books from neighbors and demonstrated a drive to change his life. Up to that time, Lincoln's understanding of grammar had been mostly self-taught, but in New Salem, he befriended the local schoolmaster, Mentor Graham. Under Graham's tutelage, Lincoln immersed himself in the study of vocabulary and grammar. Speaking publicly also became important to Lincoln, and he began attending meetings of the New Salem Debating Society.

Lincoln's drive to make something of himself yielded encouraging signs. In 1832, at age twenty-three, he announced his candidacy as a Whig for the Illinois State Legislature. He had lived in New Salem for only one year.

In the midst of that election, his local militia company chose him as captain in the Black Hawk War, an election he regarded as one of his proudest achievements. Hard work and the ambition to read and learn had already elevated him from "a piece of floating driftwood" to a viable candidate for the state legislature and a militia captain. Although Lincoln lost the legislative race in 1832, he polled 277 of New Salem's 300 votes cast. Having lost, he persisted. His confidence in personal success was increasing.

Lincoln then tried operating a general store, but it failed. Undaunted, he became the local postmaster and then a deputy surveyor, although he knew nothing about surveying. Incredibly, his ambition was so ferocious that he wound up surveying the towns of Petersburg, Bath, New Boston, Albany, and Huron, Illinois, as well as many roadways in the area. His future law partner and good friend, William Herndon, would say of Lincoln, "His ambition was a little engine that knew no rest."

On April 19, 1834, Lincoln again declared as a Whig candidate for the state legislature. He had established some credibility and a reputation for integrity. The Democrats even supported him this time, "purely out of a personal regard for him." He won the election easily. During that election, John Todd Stuart of Springfield approached Lincoln about studying law. Lincoln readily agreed and journeyed to Stuart's law office in Springfield to borrow books. He spent hours in seclusion studying and conferred with Stuart whenever he had questions, which were many.

On September 9, 1836, only five years after Lincoln first appeared in New Salem, the Illinois Supreme Court enrolled him as a member of the Illinois bar, and he became John Todd Stuart's law partner in Springfield. His success was due entirely to his drive to succeed or, as he put it, his "resolution to succeed."

He then spent ten years as a circuit lawyer, from age twenty-seven to about thirty-seven, where he rode by horseback all over southern and central Illinois representing individuals in court cases. With this broad experience in law, he made many friends and impressed everyone with his honesty, overall personal character, and his ability to speak clearly about important issues.

Through his study of American history, Lincoln became an expert on the U.S. Constitution and the Declaration of Independence, from which he realized that the phrase "all men are created equal" made it clear that slavery was not only immoral but also unlawful.

Elected to Congress in 1846, he continued to rise, gaining the Republican nomination for the United States Senate in 1858. He became president in 1860, less than thirty years after he appeared in New Salem as "a piece of floating driftwood."

Few human beings have had to suffer as many personal and political hardships as Abraham Lincoln, but he possessed a special and powerful quality that allowed him to sustain his strength, overcome these obstacles, persist after failure, and succeed. It was his "resolution to succeed," or as we call it today, his drive.

WHAT'S YOUR WHY?

"Looking back, we see with great clarity, and what once appeared as difficulties now reveal themselves as blessings."

—Unknown

There are over 6,000 books written about Abraham Lincoln, but few of them explore his inner motivations. Initially, it is clear Lincoln's childhood hardships and poverty instilled in him a strong desire to make something of himself. This was his initial "why." But he had no idea what that something was. Then he stumbled across the area of law and politics, found his strength and his calling, and began his journey to success.

Much later, as president of the United States, Lincoln saw the country he loved torn apart by slavery. His commitment to the moral and lawful necessity of ending slavery, along with his commitment to saving the Union, became Lincoln's ultimate "why," and this provided him the strength, motivation, and drive to ultimately succeed.

FINDING YOUR DRIVE

"In the end, you will be judged not by what you believed, planned, or dreamed, but by what you did."

—Unknown

We can all increase our success and happiness by understanding our "why." To get more clarity on this important motivator, ask yourself the following questions:

- What is important to you? And why?
- Why do you want to succeed?
- What do you want to do with your life? And why?

To find your "why," you usually have to look over your shoulder, looking back to your childhood and early experiences.

Reflecting on my early years and my father's failures, my initial "why" was to restore my family's dignity, which I felt we had lost. This really drove me to achieve both wealth and a good reputation. But after achieving these things by age sixty, I needed a new "why." My experience with cancer helped me find it.

THREE KEYS TO SUCCESS

"Motivation is the anticipation of success."

—Unknown

As I mentioned earlier, several years ago I had the pleasure of getting to know Bill Bonnstetter, a pioneer in the field of self-awareness and founder of Target Training International, one of the world's largest assessment companies. He had studied people, success and entrepreneurship for over forty years and had a wealth of knowledge and wisdom.

One day we were having lunch together, and I asked him what he thought were the most important attributes of successful people. He told me there were three traits that really stood out:

- Goal Achievement. The habit of setting and achieving broad goals that guide your decision making and purpose.
- Self-Management. The ability to allocate your time and resources to achieve your goals.
- Self-Direction. Confidence that you are on the right path to achieve your goals.

Coming from Bill, this was especially powerful knowledge to have. Clarity on your goals and the discipline to manage yourself generates the confidence and fuels the drive it takes to succeed.

DISCIPLINE—THE DIFFERENTIATOR

"If I had eight hours to chop down a tree, I would spend six hours sharpening my axe."

—Anonymous Woodsman

When I closed down Trammell Crow's struggling homebuilding operation in Denver back in 1990, I needed some local help. Having been active with the Lee Evans Seminar Group, where I met Dave Stone and other homebuilder consultants, I had come to know Chuck Shinn, who happened to live in Denver, so I hired him to help me out.

Chuck had worked exclusively in the housing business and specialized in helping builders focus on cost control so they could be more profitable. He had worked with hundreds of different companies and could quickly separate the good ones from the not-so-good ones. Chuck recently retired and wrote an article about his career. "Discipline is the differentiator," he said with complete confidence. "Successful builders have a system, and the discipline to follow it."

167

Discipline is one of my top twelve performance character traits. In chapter 6, I defined discipline as "having the self-control to establish and follow a regimen that leads to the accomplishment of a worthy goal." Like most personal qualities, discipline is really just a habit that you can develop and improve with practice.

Discipline is the willingness to endure short-term pain for long-term pleasure. The most accomplished athletes—like Steph Curry and Tom Brady—are marvels of discipline. They drill; they do the reps; they'll shoot 1,000 free throws or throw 500 passes a day. In doing the same thing over and over again, it becomes second nature, and they also learn certain subtleties about their skills that are beyond the reach of those who lack this discipline.

Discipline is what it takes to do deliberate practice. Hope is not a plan. And achieving your plan means getting up in the morning, making your bed, putting your boots on, picking up the ax, and starting to chop.

A COMPETITIVE SPIRIT

"Look in the mirror. That's your competition."

—Eric Thomas

As I reflect on some of the most successful people I have known (Harry Frampton, Ron Terwilliger, David Weekley, Eli Capilouto, Doug Ducey, Matt Bevin, Trammell Crow, and many others), I recognize that they have all been intense competitors. They had a drive to succeed. They all accepted a challenge, encountered adversity and resistance, persisted, endured, and competed to win. But before you can win, you need to *want* to win.

When our middle son, John, was a junior in high school, he was the star running back on the Corona del Sol football team. One late August afternoon, he was on his second practice of the day. It was especially hot that day, even for Phoenix, in the 110-degree range at 6 p.m.

At the end of practice, his team separated into positions, and I watched John and about eight or ten other offensive backs run ten forty-yard wind sprints. I could see John was trying really hard when he won the first three, and then I was astounded to see him keep the effort up and win all ten sprints!

On the way home I said, "John, did you realize that you won all ten wind sprints today?"

"Dad," he said, "I haven't lost one all summer." And he said this not out of pride but as a matter of fact. He had set a standard for himself to win, and the yardstick he used was his own. That is what I mean by a competitive spirit.

Playing sports brings this out in all of us. It requires discipline, resilience, and confidence. It's difficult, but when you've finished the race and done the best you can do, you have a deep sense of satisfaction and your self-esteem and resilience have improved.

FINDING YOUR "WHY"

"There are no traffic jams on the extra mile."

—Zig Ziglar

Finding your "why" is never easy. It often starts with some reflection and involves some trial and error. Ultimately, our most powerful goals are usually rooted in our personal history and our motivating values, as described in chapter 9 on self-awareness. Looking at my own personal motivating values, I am not surprised by them:

- Traditional: Values proven principles and ideals.
- Individualistic: Values competition and improvement.
- Utilitarian: Values wealth and efficiency.

To find your "why" and your worthy goals, it is very helpful to know and tap into your strongest motivating values. When you are doing something that is consistent with your strongest values, it is much easier to find the discipline and energy to achieve them.

Drive is certainly one of the least discussed, yet most important, prerequisites for success. To tap into this powerful motivator, you first need a strong personal commitment or resolution to succeed, and get clear on why success is important to you. Then, set inspiring personal goals and create the discipline and competitive spirit that will propel you to the finish line.

Chapter 15

MANAGE YOUR CAREER

"Time is free, but it's priceless. You can't own it, but
you can use it. You can't keep it, but you can spend it.
Once you've lost it, you can't get it back."

—Harvey McKay

When our youngest son, Michael, was a senior at the University of Arizona, I asked him about his plans after college, especially his job plans. Like most college seniors, he was distracted by college life and not at all prepared for the real world. "Dad," he said, as he began the last semester of his senior year, "I'm just too busy to think about getting a job."

On the day Mike graduated, he had no clue what to do. When pressed, the best he could come up with was, "Dad, I think I'll just move back to Phoenix and live with some friends and start looking for a job." Because Mike was our third son, I had been through this before, but as a parent, I was in full panic mode. How could this happen?

Well, after a few weeks, Mike decided he would go backpacking in South America with some friends to "de-stress" for a month or so, and when he got back he would buckle down, get serious, and get going. When he returned from the trip, he did as he planned and started job hunting—mostly on the Internet, submitting his resumé for random jobs.

He then found an interview opportunity with a popular new high-end restaurant in Scottsdale called Modern Steak, which was created by an Arizona restauranteur named Sam Fox. Mike got the job and started as a waiter.

Mike loved the job, especially being on his feet, meeting new people, winning their confidence, and trying to get a big tip! He made a game of it and would set a goal for every table he served: "How many bottles of wine can I sell them? How many desserts? How big a tip can I get?" Soon, people were coming into Modern Steak and asking for Mike. They liked him so much they would wait for one of his tables. As his dad, I was impressed by how he found this job on his own and how he was discovering his natural talents. It was a great beginning.

After about six months, Mike followed Sam Fox to a new restaurant in Newport Beach, California, and started working there, but it soon fizzled out. He had heard about a commercial brokerage opportunity in Newport Beach with a tenant representation company and sought out one of the principals, convincing the principal to give him a chance. Mike is now, at age thirty-eight, one of the top tenant rep brokers in the large Newport Beach office market and a rising star in his profession. And it all started with selling steaks.

As I often tell people, there are really only three primary areas in every company, and everyone's natural strength usually lies in only one of them:

- Operations & Management
- Finance & Accounting
- Sales & Marketing

With our three sons, we had one of each. Tommy was the operator, John the finance guy, and Mike was the natural salesman. Now in their late thirties and early forties, each of them has found his niche.

A lot of people under-optimize their career potential because they let others make their job decisions, are too slow in changing positions, and don't align their strengths and motivating values with their career paths. Managing your career success requires that you excel at your current job, prioritize learning and personal growth, and use solid judgment when it's time for a change.

JOBS AND CAREERS

"The best way to predict the future is to create it."

—Abraham Lincoln

Jobs and careers are two different things. A job can be doing anything for any length of time and may or may not lead anywhere. But a career is a series of individual jobs that progressively builds on each other, creating more knowledge, more experience, and more value in the individual.

With a twenty-year career, you can get twenty years of experience. But with a twenty-year series of disconnected jobs, you can get one year of experience twenty times, which is not very valuable for anyone.

I was recently talking with a prominent faculty member at a major university about career planning and asked him what student success meant to him. He paused for a moment, reflected on my question, and then said, "global citizenship." Really? Then he went on to promote his study abroad programs so students could explore cultural diversity and not waste their time "flipping burgers" at McDonald's. My take is that twenty years from now those "global citizens" will be working for the guy who was flipping burgers!

Many colleges love to brag about their career placement programs. In most cases, these should be called job placement programs. They may help you clean up your social media profile, put together a nice-looking resumé, and teach you a few interviewing tricks, but this is kind of like putting lipstick on a pig. It's about looking good, not *being* good. You shouldn't have to fake it when you go looking for a job. It is much better to focus on actually becoming good than it is to just try to make yourself look good.

T.W. LEWIS

THE VALUE OF WORKPLACE EXPERIENCE

"Work to become, not to acquire."

—Elbert Hubbard

Don't get me wrong. Colleges, universities, and formal education can be very valuable to their graduates, and they have their place. The people, programs, facilities, and opportunities are there. But it is up to you to take responsibility for your learning and to set your own path. If you do, you'll get off to a good start. If you don't … not so much. Way too many students leave college with crushing debt, worthless degrees, and very few real, tangible skills.

The most important lessons that prepare you for success are learned in the real world, outside of universities and classrooms, through workplace experience. Whether it's flipping burgers, waiting tables, or sweeping houses like I did after earning my MBA, these experiences help you learn how things really work, how to get things done, and how to work with others. These opportunities present themselves in entry-level jobs and in every position after that. Trammell Crow used to say, "If you want to own an office building someday, start out washing the windows."

FINDING A JOB

"Everything will be okay in the end. If it's not okay, it's not the end."

—John Lennon

Most people in the job placement industry today usually start out by focusing on the importance of networking opportunities, polishing resumés, preparing for interviews, and negotiating salaries. The goal of this approach is to make you look better than you really are by exaggerating your talent and experience to make you seem more dynamic and employable. This is artificial, and it doesn't work.

Probably the biggest obstacle to finding a job when you don't have one is fear—fear of failure, fear of rejection, and fear of taking the wrong job. Many times I have seen people frozen with fear as they sought the perfect

174

job to fit their passion. Following your passion is certainly the worst career advice I have ever heard.

There are no perfect jobs, and the only person (other than you) who really cares about your passion (at the moment) is probably your mother. So if you are just getting started, take the first decent opportunity—even if it's flipping burgers, selling steaks, or washing windows. If you work hard and pay attention, you can end up owning the place.

KEEPING A JOB

"To be a leader you have to earn the trust of others. Trust is the natural result of trustworthiness."

—Dennis Prager

Once you have found a job, there are a few basics worth pointing out that will ensure you keep it and advance in responsibility and compensation. As the owner of a company for twenty years and employer of about 100 people at any one time, I can assure you that good bosses pay attention to how different people perform, and the executive team spends a lot of time discussing this because, well, performance matters.

The six general rules for excelling at your job are pretty clear:

1. Put in the expected amount of effort, plus about 20 percent.

2. Exceed expectations. Get things done. Hustle.

3. Do what you say you will do when you say you will do it.

4. Get along with your boss. Adapt to his or her style.

5. Figure out the culture, and adapt to fit in.

6. Add value to your employer in excess of your compensation.

Rule number four, getting along with your boss and adapting to his or her style, may strike some people the wrong way, because they may believe the boss should adapt to them. It doesn't work that way. Your boss is your customer, and it's your job to keep your customer happy. And it's in your best interest, too. Getting along with your boss is an important part of managing your career.

From an employer's standpoint, firing employees is never easy. But the reality is that there are A, B, C, and D performers. I've never really had much luck in coaching underperformers, so spending time developing the top 25 percent is usually much more productive. In a competitive world, not everyone is going to make the cut. There is usually a time to leave any company, but you always want to do it on your terms, not theirs.

CHANGING JOBS

"Accomplished people come to wisdom through failure.
We get very little wisdom from success."

—Unknown

When a person walks into my office and tells me she has decided to leave, I am always disappointed because I feel that we have let her down. But the first words out of my mouth are "Congratulations!" I say this because I know that deciding to leave your job for another, hopefully better opportunity, is the toughest and most critical part of managing a successful career.

From my experience, most jobs go like this:

- Year one—I love my job.

- Year two—I like my job.

- Year three—There are several things I don't like about my job.

- Year four—There are a lot of things I don't like about my job.

- Year five—I need to find another job.

Rule number one in changing jobs is, "Don't leave the old one until you get the new one." It is much easier to get one when you have one. Being unemployed usually raises questions for the new employer. And they like the idea of being able to take another company's best performers.

Because the average mid-career job will last three to five years, it is important for you to exercise good judgment when selecting your new company, and especially your new boss. And remember to always emphasize the opportunity to learn and grow when evaluating your options.

And equally important, always leave your current employer on good terms, and don't ever burn any bridges. It is common for the people you have worked with in the past to be instrumental in your future career. You might even have the opportunity to work with them again, and your reputation will always follow you.

CAREER-PLANNING MODELS

"If you chase two rabbits, you will catch neither."

—Russian proverb

There are actually some concrete career-planning models and principles broadly known in business circles that are not being taught to undergraduate college students anywhere in America, to my knowledge. This is unfortunate, even inexcusable, given its importance. Most colleges today offer dozens of courses on topics like "The Impact of Music on the Middle-Eastern Conflict" but not one course on career planning. That needs to change.

To address this problem, our T.W. Lewis Foundation recently made a grant to an educational nonprofit called Indigo (the assessment company referenced in chapter 9) to create a one-credit class in self-awareness and career readiness. Our plan is to offer this course free of charge to any college or university. I invite you to take this course, which also includes a comprehensive Indigo assessment that helps you better understand your behaviors, motivating values, and strengths. Just go to: **www.indigoeducationcompany.com/solidground**. Here are two of the career-planning models discussed in the course:

- Target Model
- Functional Area Model

Target Model

If you know the industry in which you want to work, the target model is very simple. In hindsight, it is actually the model I followed in my career.

	TIME IN JOB	OBJECTIVE
Job #1	2 years	Get on the target in the right industry.
Job #2	2 years	Find another job better suited to your strengths and values.
Job #3	3 to 5 years	Keep learning and growing.
Job #4	3 to 5 years	Keep learning and growing.
Job #5	Bull's-eye	By now, you will be in a job that is a great fit for you.

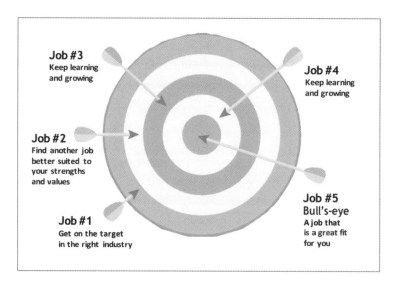

Career Planning Target Model

You will notice that the amount of time I have ideally allocated to each job, progressively increasing the time to allow your learning and growing to go deeper as you mature. In this model, after four jobs and only fourteen years out of college, you are still only thirty-six years old with a lot of experience in multiple roles. And, you will have created a lot of value for yourself and your long term career.

Functional Area Model

In case you're not really sure which industry you like, you can define your target as one of the three functional areas that exists in all organizations:

- Operations & Management
- Finance & Accounting
- Sales & Marketing

Finding your bull's-eye here is a process similar to that of the target model. You start by just getting an entry-level job in your selected functional area, and progress steadily from there.

ENTREPRENEURIAL SUCCESS—WHAT IT REALLY TAKES

Another career option is to be an entrepreneur and work for yourself. But this is not easy. It took me eighteen years to feel prepared enough to be successful with this option. Individuals who are able to start large companies (over $50 million a year in sales) are rare, but if you have the drive, you are halfway there. The other half is preparing yourself to succeed.

Entrepreneurship is getting a lot of love these days, and for good reason. The speed of change in all areas is occurring at such a pace that old ways are quickly becoming obsolete, creating new opportunities in every sector for those with ambition, skills, and the personal characteristics that are necessary for entrepreneurial success.

We all know that an entrepreneur needs to understand the customer, have basic business skills, and be able to communicate his or her vision. But little is said in popular writings or college entrepreneurship courses about the basic personality and value characteristics that correlate best with successful entrepreneurs. Much of the popular literature on the subject focuses on teamwork, passion, creativity, and other soft skills, but there's also a lot of hard behavioral evidence showing that most successful entrepreneurs have a predictable pattern of behaviors and values that has little correlation to teamwork or passion.

Based on my observation and experience, I have learned the most important personal qualities of a successful entrepreneur include the following three specific behavioral traits and three motivating values:

- Behavioral traits:
    - Assertive. You are both dominant and persuasive, and are driven to solve problems and overcome obstacles.
    - Fast-paced. You like a lot of action and change.
    - Persistent. You are resilient, won't quit, and love the grind.
- Motivating values:
    - Utilitarian. You value efficiency and return on investment, don't like to waste anything, and are motivated by economics.
    - Individualistic. You see yourself as a person who makes things happen. You are constantly improving, like to compete and are motivated by recognition.
    - Theoretical. You are motivated by knowledge and love to learn new things.

Although these traits can correlate to entrepreneurial success, there are still many intangible qualities of the human spirit that are not measurable and can make a huge difference. Ultimately, if you're an entrepreneur, you have to work hard, initiate, take risks, and be very good at what you do. The rewards will accrue in direct relationship to the value you bring your customers—just ask Bill Gates and Mark Zuckerberg.

SOLID GROUND

Before you invest your time in trying to be an entrepreneur, consider the business skills (like accounting and people management) that take most of us a while to learn. At their core, entrepreneurs are independent businesspeople who must plan, organize, motivate, and control.

Entrepreneurs also have to initiate new things and have the drive to overcome all the obstacles in the way—and there are always many obstacles! Then, they have to take personal and financial risks—calculated risks—that will make most people uncomfortable. Here are some of the advantages and disadvantages of being an entrepreneur:

Advantages

- You have a great boss—you!
- You set the agenda.
- You make the decisions.
- You can customize the business around your skills and dreams.
- You can create jobs and careers for others.
- You can improve your community and the world.

Disadvantages

- You have few days off.
- You can't quit.
- It takes a lot of work—a minimum of sixty hours per week.
- It's risky—you might go broke.
- It's not easy. There are a lot of struggles along the way.
- It takes a long time to realize the dream.

Five Phases of Entrepreneurial Success

1. Vision. Must be clear and noble.
2. Struggle. Can't avoid it—can be ten years.
3. Journey. Takes a long time—the second ten years.
4. Passion. Increases along the way.
5. Purpose. Often discovered at the end.

ENTREPRENEURIAL SUCCESS—MYTHS AND REALITIES

MYTH	REALITY
It's about great ideas.	It's about solving a market problem.
It's about the team.	It's about the leader.
It's about passion.	It's about adding value for customers.
It's about strategy.	It's about execution.
It's about growth.	It's about constant improvement.

CAREER EXECUTION—A SUMMARY

"The bad news is that time flies. The good news is that you're the pilot."

—Michael Altschuler

I have looked at dozens of books on career management, and most of them are not very good. My favorite is *The Pathfinder* (1998) by Nicholas Lore. The author accurately describes the career process as a journey of discovery in which *you* are the one in charge—hands on the steering wheel—as you drive down your career path. And this is the best way to approach it.

When it comes to taking responsibility for your career success, I like the idea of finding role models over mentors. The word mentor seems to imply that it is the mentor's job to teach the student. I never really felt like I had a mentor, but I had lots of role models—usually my senior executives— that I respected, watched closely, and then tried to emulate. But they were never responsible for teaching me; I was responsible for learning. There's a big difference.

MAKING AND KEEPING COMMITMENTS

"Talent is God-given; be humble. Fame is man-given; be thankful. Conceit is self-given; be careful."

—John Wooden

One of the most important things you can do in life and in business is to earn the trust of others. The best way to do this is simply to make and then keep your commitments. When you do this, you make a deposit into your "trust account," and when you fail to make and keep your promises, you make a withdrawal. These choices are cumulative. The goal is to build a big positive trust account balance, and you will become widely trusted and respected. Nothing in your career is more important than being worthy of trust.

In closing this chapter, I just can't overemphasize the value of making friends as you progress along your career path. And once you've made them, it is important to keep them. Had I not developed trust with Ron Terwilliger and Dick Michaux from my Sea Pines days, I would never have had the opportunity to join Trammell Crow ten years later. And had I not made friends with David Weekley, John Johnson, and Jim Rado while we battled it out in Denver in the early 1980s, I would not have been able to call them in 2012 and make the deal to sell my homebuilding business to them. As I've said many times, you can only do business with friends, enemies, or strangers, so making and keeping friends is always the best way to manage your career, and your life.

PART IV

LIFE'S GREATEST ACHIEVEMENTS

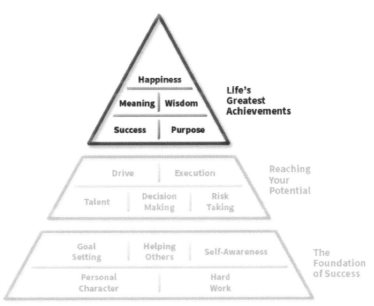

The Achiever's Model

Chapter 16

ACHIEVE SUCCESS

"There are no secrets to success, so don't waste your time looking for them. Success is the result of perfection, hard work, learning from failure, and persistence."

—Colin Powell

In these last five chapters, I want to share what I believe are the five greatest achievements of a well-lived life. These are my own thoughts based on what I've learned from my experience, from reading and studying these subjects, and from the ideas of many of the great leaders and thinkers I admire.

I certainly don't want to present myself as a philosopher. Being a homebuilder, real estate developer, and philanthropist doesn't leave much time for contemplating the philosophical. By temperament, I've always been more concerned with doing tangible things—like building houses and solving problems.

But success, purpose, meaning, wisdom, and happiness are also tangible, even if you can't measure them the way you can measure customer satisfaction or return on investment. That's why I call them, collectively, life's greatest achievements. It's what we all hope for and ultimately want. Sharing my philosophy about them is a part of my philanthropy, which makes sense because both of these words have the same root in the Greek word for love—philosophy being the "love of wisdom" and philanthropy the "love of mankind."

Success is the progressive realization of a worthy ideal. We all have many successes and failures in our lives, but they are never permanent. Some people have a lot more success than others because they are more talented, more driven, more disciplined, and work harder. To truly be successful, we need to continue to pursue worthy ideals in all facets of our lives, including personal, family, friendships, and career.

A WORTHY IDEAL

"Success is the progressive realization of a worthy ideal."

—Earl Nightingale

Earl Nightingale was a famous radio personality, author, and speaker. His definition of success as the "progressive realization of a worthy ideal" is the best I have ever heard. I love its emphasis on progress—on moving forward continuously toward your end. And I love, too, his insistence that your goal has to be a *worthy* one. If we were to say a day trader was having great success with his goal of maximizing his daily profits, we would be using the term only in a superficial sense. Real success requires the presence of a noble goal—a worthy ideal.

Earl grew up during the Great Depression. His dad left his family when he was only six, forcing Earl's mom and siblings to live in a tent city outside Long Beach, California. An industrious young man, Earl did whatever he could to support his family, finding his way to radio just before he joined the U.S. Marine Corps. He was in Pearl Harbor on the fateful day of December 7, 1941—one of just twelve Marines to survive the sinking of the USS *Arizona*.

After serving for the duration of World War II, he returned to work in radio. Later, he bought an insurance business, became an internationally renowned speaker and author, and in 1957, wrote one of the great motivational works of all time, *The Strangest Secret*.

I can identify with a lot of Earl's story, but what struck me the most about his approach to motivating others was his emphasis on *clearly visualizing your goal*. He said that to obtain your "worthy ideal," you had to get your thinking right.

OPEN TO EXPERIENCE

"The road to success is traveled by those who believe in themselves."

—Unknown

One of the reasons I thought it was important to tell my personal story in chapters 1 through 5 was to demonstrate how open I have been to new places, new people, and new ideas. Years ago, I was talking with an old college friend from UK. He had stayed in Kentucky after graduation, and he said, "You know, Tom, it seems like the people who left Kentucky have done better than those who stayed." He was generally right, but it's not because there wasn't opportunity in our home state. It was because those who left tended to be more open to new opportunities.

From Utah to Rhode Island, to Florida and Kentucky, to North Carolina and Virginia, and then to Ohio and finally Arizona, I have always chosen new experiences over familiarity. As my friend Dr. Lee Todd, former president of the University of Kentucky, once said to students, it is best to "choose challenge over comfort." That's being open to experience. People who make that choice tend to achieve more.

The fear of failure really does hold many people back and can be extremely hard to overcome. But overcoming this fear just once—forcing yourself to make the leap for the first time—makes every successive leap a bit easier. The secret is hard work. Hard work makes it easier to "choose challenge" because it creates competence. Competence leads to confidence, and confidence makes it easier to overcome fear.

In short, being open to experience means saying "yes" to new things. Making mistakes, learning, growing, and improving—that is *always* the path to success. Openness to new things also includes using your imagination, cultivating a wide variety of interests, and knowing that any failure will only be temporary. As the saying goes, "Don't be afraid to fail. Everyone else has."

FOCUS AND HARD WORK

"The only place success comes before work is in the dictionary."

—T.W. Lewis

I talked earlier about how the words construction and investment had a strong appeal to me even as a young man when I didn't have much knowledge or experience. What I did have was the ability to focus on my goals, to look for opportunities, and to work as hard or harder than anyone else because I wanted to succeed.

Whether it was playing high school football or running a jackhammer, I learned early that working hard was its own reward. This work ethic served me well in school, leading me to a scholarship to the University of Kentucky, where I would learn not only about engineering but more about leadership and myself.

I also naturally learned discipline, mostly by just doing the work. I learned I was good at picking up new ideas and making them my own. James Allen's *As a Man Thinketh* (1903) made a deep impression on me, especially his message, "Thoughts lead to actions. Actions lead to habits. Habits lead to character, and character leads to destiny." Allen wrote his classic book eighteen years before Earl Nightingale's birth, and Nightingale took this same idea and brought it to a much wider audience.

As I continued to learn more about myself and my strengths and talents, I decided to focus on business and construction, which took me to the University of North Carolina. In Chapel Hill, Dr. Gerry Bell helped me understand the need to think clearly. His insights on achievement, personality types, and the importance of having a balanced view of myself, others, and the world were foundational for me. This was my beginning.

SELF-AWARENESS

"I cannot give you the formula for success, but I can give you the formula for failure—try to please everybody."

—Unknown

My experience in college and graduate school taught me that another component of right thinking and, therefore, success is self-awareness. "Know thyself" was already a common saying in the Greek world by the time Plato used it in his dialogues. His method wasn't to devise a system like his student Aristotle did or to list wise sayings as other philosophers did. He wrote dialogues in which the characters debated the meaning of important ideas like the virtues or how to organize a society. His main character in most of the dialogues was Socrates, the voice of his own teacher. And when it came to the debates, Socrates usually won.

But I think this saying has another meaning. Know who you are, what your strengths are, and where you're weak. Don't waste time on what others think of you. As Dr. Bell would say: Accept the reality of yourself, of others, and of all things as they really are, and then get to work making the changes in the world you feel called to make. As my friend David Weekley says, "A leader defines reality and provides hope."

The world is filled with dreamers who have unrealistic views of their real abilities or romantic ideas about their callings. Many more people are too pessimistic about their talents and opportunities. Some people idealize the glamorous lives of celebrities and end up thinking too little of themselves by comparison. They measure their reality against the illusions of Hollywood or Instagram and find their lives wanting. Envying someone you don't know well is the opposite of self-knowledge.

Knowing yourself is about knowing reality and your place in it, and the best way to figure those things out is to work hard and be open to new opportunities. Knowing yourself isn't just about knowing your limitations; it's about knowing your potential and where you want to go—your worthy ideal. So pay attention to your thoughts. "Thoughts lead to actions. Actions lead to habits." The rest is history.

SETTING GOALS

"Luck is what happens when preparation meets opportunity."

—Seneca

The more you know about yourself, the easier it is to discover what you want to do and, more importantly, who you want to become. This is where goals come in. In chapter 8, I shared some of the popular and successful models for setting goals and added my own model for goal-setting. There is no getting around it; if you want your desired future to become real, you *have* to set goals.

When I went to UK to study mechanical engineering, I always went to class and did my homework. But as I got closer to completing the program and attaining my goal, I learned more about my abilities and what I didn't want to do, adjusting my expectations and setting the next goal of success in a graduate business program. As I neared that goal, I started to see other possibilities and I set my "someday" goal—my big life vision for what I wanted to become. This clear vision became my North Star, and guided me for the next forty years.

The immediate result of getting my MBA at UNC is that it prepared me to join an outstanding group of fellow MBAs at Sea Pines. Because I had been working hard, I had the confidence to step into the new corporate environment and not be intimidated by my bosses or new colleagues. I belonged among them because I had earned it.

With Sea Pines, Ryan, UDC, and Trammell Crow, I continued my journey, progressively learning all the skills it would take to run my own company. Eighteen years later, the opportunity presented itself, and my "root structure" was in place. It was all made possible by having a clear "someday" goal.

The success I have had would not have been possible without goals—and without adjusting them. Goals don't guarantee success, but they help you set priorities on the road to success. Goals become the roadmap you use to get where you want to go. If you're competitive, these goals tend to instill the drive necessary to overcome obstacles and achieve success.

SOLID GROUND

MINDSET

"We like to think of our champions and idols as superheroes who were born different from us. We don't like to think of them as relatively ordinary people who made themselves extraordinary."

—Carol Dweck

I'm careful not to engage in "talent worship," as if there is some magic trait that winners have and losers don't. Talent is important, and it is a key ingredient for success, but talent is not enough. When you see a truly great athlete (or businessman, or surgeon, or salesperson) succeeding year after year, what you're actually seeing is the result of ambition, character, natural gifts, and tens of thousands of hours of hard work.

Consider the work of Stanford psychologist Carol S. Dweck. In her book *Mindset: The New Psychology of Success* (2006), Dweck pulled together a huge amount of scientific research from various fields to try to figure out why some people succeed and others don't. Among the many insights Dweck shares in this influential book are those she gained from her analysis of the careers and language of some of the most famous athletes. There are countless stories of talented players bursting onto the scene—excelling in college and flaming out quickly at the professional level. Many of these players had exceptional natural gifts, and many of them worked hard to get the success they had. Yet it didn't last.

What separates these players from the greats, writes Dweck, was their *mindset*, especially their response to failures and setbacks. Those with a "fixed" mindset tended to prize raw talent above all else, thinking of their traits as immutable and unchangeable. When they failed, they saw it as proof of their limits. They were not able to go any further.

Those with a "growth" mindset, even if they had the same or lesser abilities, saw their failures as *temporary*, as proof of their need to improve in a particular way. Growth mindset players saw themselves as being able to improve and adapt, no matter what. They were open to experience, one of the key traits of achievers.

DRIVE AND GRIT

"Enthusiasm is common. Endurance is rare."

—Angela Duckworth

Psychologist Angela Duckworth expands on the growth mindset in her book *Grit: The Power of Passion and Perseverance* (2016), where she offers a simple calculation based on her extensive research on success. Here is what she came up with:

Talent x Effort = Skill
Skill x Effort = Achievement

By this formula—which she derived from her study of the experiences of many top performers—effort has twice the impact as talent and skill. And, of course, they all reinforce each other. Dr. Duckworth argues you have the power to control effort, or hard work, and to "grow your grit." How do you do this? She offers four steps:

1. Develop a fascination: You have to be inspired if you are going to persevere.

2. Daily improvement: Try to beat your own best. "Whatever it takes, I want to improve."

3. Remind yourself of your highest purpose: If you can keep your purpose in mind, you will be more resilient in the face of setbacks.

4. Adopt a growth mindset: Do all you can to develop a healthy, positive response to setbacks, seeing opportunity for growth where others see defeat.

A gritty approach is obviously important for success, but I want to point out one more thing: *you have to know you can improve.* This has to be a fundamental belief, not just a hope and a prayer. As the sportscaster Jimmy Dykes says, "Hope is not a plan."

SOLID GROUND

Belief itself will not make you an all-American or the best executive in your company, but it can make it possible for you to succeed in your field. Self-knowledge is important, and paying attention to your natural gifts is also important. But as I've been saying throughout this chapter and throughout this book, clear thinking about where you want to be only leads to success if you are also willing to learn from your mistakes and continually improve through extra effort.

A SUCCESSFUL LIFE

"The toughest thing about success is that you've got to keep on being a success."

—Irving Berlin

I have long admired John Wooden, who is still the most successful college basketball coach of all time. By the time he retired from coaching at UCLA, he had won more than 80 percent of his games and ten national championships. More than forty years after his retirement, no one else is even close to reaching these achievements.

How could he be so successful for so long when he was constantly working with new players year after year? He may have been one of the all-time best at developing a *system* that he could share with others, letting them come into a winning organization where they could thrive. Coach Wooden was continuously improving—something he also expected of his players. He left as little as possible to chance, and a big part of this system was his approach to discipline.

What is so interesting about Coach Wooden is how successful he was while almost never talking about winning. He was a master at knowing and accepting himself, his players, and the reality of the world in which they all operated. He saw all the moving parts, and he had a lot of talented players, but his real goal went far beyond just winning basketball games. He thought about how his teams could best thrive together, ultimately concluding that thriving depended on friendship, collaboration, unselfishness, hard work, and a sense of shared purpose.

In other words, Wooden was concerned with character. I talked earlier about the traits that define one's character, distinguishing the performance traits such as achievement, assertiveness, competence, discipline, and perseverance, from the moral traits, such as compassion, courage, decency, faith, and generosity. Wooden understood all of this. He was as great a teacher of character as he was of basketball.

Now it's true that many great performers don't really have all the important moral virtues. We've seen a number of them fall from grace not by losing their drive but because of a serious moral failing. If you want to be successful, you have to be honest about what is holding you back—whether it's performance traits or moral traits. As Brian Kelly, the head football coach at Notre Dame, said, "Before we can start winning, we have to stop losing."

But these observations about character and success point to something even more important, which is that success in business, or sports, or life does not, in the end, lead to happiness. As I discuss in chapter 20, true happiness depends more on moral character and less on success or winning. Great leaders understand this.

John Wooden was one of those great leaders. To him, victory was important, but it was the result of something that was even more important: personal character. As successful as he was on the court, his greatest legacy lies in the love and admiration so many had for him—and, I would add, in his example and writings on leadership and teamwork.

All the authors and leaders I have mentioned in this book believe that real and sustained success requires having the right "mindset." And the right mindset includes a strong sense of character. The ultimate importance of character is rarely clear at first, but it becomes more clear along the journey, seeing us through both victories and defeats.

Chapter 17

DISCOVER PURPOSE

"Don't ask yourself what the world needs. Ask yourself what
makes you come alive, and go do that, because what
the world needs is people who have come alive."

—Howard Thurman

Philosopher, theologian, educator, and civil rights leader Howard
Thurman is not as well known today as he should be. He inspired
Martin Luther King Jr. and countless other champions of nonvi-
olent social change while writing more than twenty books and delivering
thousands of sermons and speeches. His long list of achievements is even
more remarkable considering that, as an African American, he was born in
1899 and grew up during a period of racial segregation, tension, and social
change. When we talk about having a growth mindset, of knowing how to
respond to adversity, we could hardly find a better example than Howard
Thurman.

I mention this remarkable man because of his life of purpose and his
talent for putting a great deal of wisdom into a short statement. I can't
think of a better definition of purpose than "what makes you come alive."

PURPOSE FOLLOWS TALENT

"The two most important days in your life are the day you were born and the day you find out why."

—Mark Twain

Socrates was born in 470 BC in Athens and spent his entire life there. Socrates was widely considered a people person, someone who was full of charisma and was "impossible not to like and hard not to love." His personal needs and tastes were minimal, and he never even had a job. He needed very little to be happy.

To Socrates, everything was rational, not emotional, and his strongest talent was his ability to find truth through interrogation. In his twenties, he realized science was not for him, because he was intrigued by people. He spent his days wandering the streets of Athens, talking with strangers and asking them questions. Exploring the internal world of man was his gift, and he decided to dedicate his life to it.

Socrates' special talent was his ability to charm anyone while asking tough questions—before proceeding to even tougher follow-up questions— all to get to the truth on any topic. But he didn't realize this was his special talent until he was forty years old.

Ultimately, Socrates followed his talent and became the father of Greek philosophy and, arguably, of all philosophy. His gift for exploring truth through inquiry became known as the Socratic method—a method we still use today. He was a man who truly found his purpose.

SOLID GROUND

PURPOSE FOLLOWS ADVERSITY

"Resolve to be tender with the young, compassionate with the aged, sympathetic with the striving, and tolerant of the weak and the wrong. Sometime in life you will have been all of these."

—George Washington Carver

As Socrates discovered 2,400 years ago, purpose can come in many forms. Sometimes it comes in the form of gifts—our blessings. But just as often it comes in the form of difficulties—our burdens.

In his book *Kept Afloat by a Millstone* (2000), Gordon McKeeman tells many stories about how caring for a disabled child or an elderly friend or dealing with a life-threatening disease can deepen your sensitivities and appreciation for life. Accepting our toughest life challenges can keep us going. In McKeeman's term, it can keep us afloat—and give our lives real purpose.

Mother Teresa discovered her purpose in the crowded streets of Kolkata, India, among the poorest of the poor. Many of these poor souls had been left to die in gutters and alleys, abandoned by all except Mother Teresa and her Missionaries of Charity. What began as an incredibly difficult act of love led to the realization of her purpose and the establishment of hundreds of centers of care around the world.

During his presidency, Ronald Reagan found purpose in liberating hundreds of millions of people from the threat of communism. He discovered this purpose in what might seem like the unlikeliest of places—as a leader of the Screen Actors Guild in the 1940s and 1950s. As a liberal movie star and labor leader, he saw firsthand how communism had infiltrated much of Hollywood and sought to undermine American values. His work with other union leaders to defend the United States led him to a political career that took him to the most powerful leadership position in the world. His famous resolve against communism and his legacy came from the challenges he had faced earlier in his career.

Unlike Mother Teresa and President Reagan, author J.D. Vance has a backstory to which I can relate, at least to some extent. Vance grew up in the Appalachian region of Kentucky and Ohio, where he suffered from poverty, addiction, and loss of hope. Raised by his grandparents after his mother became addicted to drugs, he joined the U.S. Marines, serving his country before enrolling at Ohio State University, where his intellectual gifts could develop. By the time he made it to Yale Law School, he had begun reckoning with his difficult childhood, and a professor encouraged him to tell his story. *Hillbilly Elegy*, his memoir, was probably the most talked-about nonfiction book of 2016, even appearing in political discussions about why many Americans felt disconnected from the American Dream.

The lesson on purpose from Mother Teresa, Ronald Reagan, and J. D. Vance is clear: Look first to the adversity you've experienced, and then use your talents to find your purpose.

PURPOSE CHANGES

"Believe in something big! Your life is worth a noble motive."

—Walter Alexander

Trying to figure out what your purpose is can be a daunting task, one that can often lead to confusion, anxiety, or both. One important thing to remember is that purpose *evolves*. As I reflect on the seven decades of my life, I believe I actually had a different purpose in each decade. It went like this:

AGE	PURPOSE
0–10	Learn to walk, talk, read, and think.
11–20	Learn to have relationships and get along with other people.
21–30	Learn to be independent and responsible. Find my strengths.
31–40	Start a family and advance my career.
41–50	Grow a family and start a company.
51–60	Transition from family to empty-nester and from business to philanthropy.
61–70	Find humility, gratitude, faith, and happiness.
71–80	To be determined …

In other words, your purpose is rarely constant. It changes as you age, mature, and encounter life's unexpected turns. As Steve Jobs said in his Stanford University graduation speech, "You can only connect the dots looking backwards." Purpose is a lot like passion in that it reveals itself more at the end than in the beginning. This is another reason why finding your talent, which is constant, will likely have longer-lasting impact than finding your passion, which can change like the wind.

Finding your purpose is not easy or simple. Understanding your purpose means knowing why you are here and what you are meant to do. As you experience new things, you will grow, change, and evolve, and the challenges you face in each phase of your life will provide you with opportunities for discovering purpose. Likely, you will not understand your ultimate purpose until late in your journey.

THE FIVE WHYS

"The purpose of life is to be useful, to be responsible, to be honorable, to help others, to stand for something, to learn, to grow, and to strive to be the best that you can be. That is the purpose of life."

—T.W. Lewis

I once heard about another interesting way to explore your purpose that was "Socratic" in that it asks five questions to get to the truth:

QUESTION	SAMPLE ANSWER
Why are you here?	To achieve and connect.
Why is it important to achieve and connect?	Because it brings out our best and builds relationships.
Why is it important to be our best and build relationships?	Because we should strive to reach our God-given potential and love others.
Why is it important to reach our God-given potential and love others?	Because each of us was put on this earth for a reason, and loving others makes a better world.
Why is that important?	Because it's the purpose of life!

This "Socratic method" is a great exercise for exploring your purpose. You may be surprised by some of your answers, but they will probably point you in the right direction.

THE ULTIMATE PURPOSE

"If you want to know your calling, you need to know your caller."

—Christian saying

I have found purpose in raising a family, building a company, and trying to help other people. Ultimately, as a Christian, I believe my highest purpose on earth is to serve God and love others. The Apostle Paul makes this clear in 1 Corinthians 12:1–11, where he talks about the "spiritual gifts" that each of us possesses and how these talents will be reflected in our purpose. No two people are exactly the same, but collectively we approach His ultimate purpose.

When I realized how God has worked in my life to give me special gifts and then put me in certain situations, I have learned that *my* purpose is really *His purpose for me*. Finding this out was a powerful moment, a great consolation, and also a challenge. I have come to believe that God has a purpose for all of us and He will help us find it.

WHAT'S YOUR PURPOSE?

"Where there is vision, there is hope."

—Unknown

As I discussed in chapter 4, when I began my company in 1991, I knew I was embarking on an important mission, and I needed some clear "guardrails" to keep me on track. So I developed a little plastic card for everyone in the company to keep in their pockets that would provide clarity on our purpose. We defined our purpose along these four distinct dimensions:

- Our style. How we treated our customers and each other.

- Our differences. How we were different from our competition.

- Our core values. Our guiding principles.

- Our purpose. Why we existed.

This little plastic card provided all the clarity and inspiration that we needed to explain:

- Who we were. Our style.

- Who we weren't. Our uniqueness.

- What we stood for. Our values.

- And why we were here. Our purpose.

The success we created at T.W. Lewis Company would not have happened had we not maintained a clear sense of purpose. And this clarity attracted a great team of people who were in alignment with our mission and our purpose.

Fifteen years later—with a lot of hard work, many mistakes, continuous improvement, and a common commitment to a worthy ideal—we achieved our goals and realized our purpose. We also survived the inevitable and brutal market downturn in 2008 because our values and our purpose were clear and strong.

EXERCISE 5: PURPOSE

Every successful CEO knows that their company needs a clear vision and purpose. But wouldn't it be just as important, and just as powerful, for every individual to also have this same clarity about their purpose with answers to these questions?

- Who you are?—Six ways you treat others
- Who you aren't?—Six unique differences
- What you stand for?—Six core values
- Why you are here?—Twenty-five words or less

I challenge you to write your own purpose statement by answering these four questions, because they will provide both the guardrails and the North Star to guide you on your journey. But remember, finding your purpose takes patience, because it will evolve over many years.

Chapter 18

CREATE MEANING

"What we obtain too cheap, we esteem too lightly. It is dearness only that gives everything its value."

—Thomas Paine

IS IT MEANINGFUL?

In his book *Happiness Is a Serious Problem* (1998), Dennis Prager makes it clear there is a strong connection among purpose, meaning, and happiness:

> Happiness can be attained under virtually any circumstances, providing you believe that your life has meaning and purpose.
>
> … To be a happy person, it is necessary to ask before acting. "Is it meaningful?" The problem, of course, is that any good action or meaningful behavior is rarely the most enticing of our choices—which only proves that the greatest battle for purpose, meaning, and happiness is with our own nature.

Before we explore the question of meaning, we need to address two beliefs. The first belief relates to transcendent meaning and asks, "Does life itself have meaning?" The second belief relates to personal meaning and asks, "Does *my* life have meaning?" While you don't necessarily have to answer each of these questions affirmatively, it makes sense for me to believe both— and I do. When I look at a newborn baby or look out my window and see the beauty and perfection of nature, it is impossible for me to believe that this earth and all its inhabitants are just the random outcomes of blind physical, chemical, and biological processes.

One more clarification before we move on: Although purpose and meaning are often used interchangeably, they are actually two different things, with meaning being the natural joy and satisfaction we experience as we follow our values and *discover* our purpose.

Creating meaning in life is very personal for each of us. It begins by accepting that we have both the freedom and the responsibility to choose "who" we are and "how" we will live. We can only find meaning by doing the things that are meaningful to us, individually, and we have to search for these things. To find real meaning, it is best to look outside of ourselves in the areas of family, career, community, and faith. We can also find meaning in living our values, embracing differences, doing hard things, and even in suffering.

MAN'S SEARCH FOR MEANING

"Life is a journey of the heart that requires the head.
Not the other way around."

—Unknown

Despite 2,500 years of pondering by philosophers, theologians, and many other great thinkers, there is still no universally accepted answer to this question, "What is the meaning of life?"

Three of the most influential thinkers of the past 150 years put forth their theories of life's meaning: German psychologist Sigmund Freud believed humans were primarily motivated by sex, no matter how much they pretended or disguised their motives; German economist Karl Marx contended that people were primarily motivated by economic forces; and Austrian psychotherapist and Holocaust survivor Viktor Frankl believed the essence of humanity could be found in man's search for meaning.

Frankl examined this search in his book *Man's Search for Meaning.* Originally published in German in 1946, and in English in 1959, this book has more than twelve million copies in print worldwide. For Frankl, meaning came from a personal commitment and a sense of responsibility to search for it.

WHAT IS MEANING?

"Don't care too much about what others think of you, but act in ways that will make you proud."

—Unknown

Frankl's emphasis on the *search* for meaning is valuable. Although there are many roads to purpose and meaning, there is a caveat—those roads must lead to something worthy. Or perhaps it would be better to say that we must be motivated in our search by a worthy ideal—like truth, justice, fairness, or charity.

For example, becoming the best surgeon, broker, homebuilder, or fire-fighter in your community are all perfectly worthy ideals. Becoming the richest or most popular person is probably not. And while no worthy ideal may ever be fully realized or completed, the very pursuit of it provides us with meaning.

To embark on a *worthy* search then is what we must do to find meaning. We must ask ourselves the big questions:

- What is worth striving for?
- What makes life worth living?
- What do you value?
- What really matters?

Once you can clearly and honestly answer these questions, it is likely that you will find meaning in their pursuit.

T.W. LEWIS

WHAT REALLY MATTERS

"It is very difficult to have a meaningful life without meaningful work."

—Jim Collins

A contemporary scholar I deeply admire is Charles Murray, who recently retired from the American Enterprise Institute. As a sociologist who focused on researching and writing about social change in America, Murray published several significant books, including *Losing Ground: American Social Policy, 1950–1980* (1984); *Coming Apart: The State of White America, 1960–2010* (2012); and *The Curmudgeon's Guide to Getting Ahead* (2014).

Murray's research aims to reveal the root causes of many of the disturbing trends that began in America in 1960, and continue today. Among these trends, of particular concern is the reduction in marriage rates, the increase in out-of-wedlock births, the increase in able men not seeking work, the decrease in community engagement, the decrease in church attendance and the resulting decrease in happiness.

By analyzing these changes, along with their correlation with increases in opioid addiction, foster children, isolation, and loneliness, Murray concludes there are only four areas of life where a person can find real meaning:

- Family: Love, marriage, and children.
- Career: Meaningful work.
- Community: Engagement and close relationships.
- Faith: Belief and active engagement.

These four areas are broad enough to include many things but specific enough to be helpful in beginning and pursuing *your* search for meaning.

SOLID GROUND

MEANING FOLLOWS PURPOSE

"The greatest joy in life is to begin."

—African proverb

Anyone over the age of fifty who has had the blessing of raising children will tell you it was certainly one of the most meaningful things they have ever done. They will also say it wasn't easy. But why is raising your children so meaningful?

When Jan and I married, we knew we wanted to have children. Jan had one little brother, Bill, and I had one older sister, Karen. We had both been raised in family environments with plenty of love, and although they were imperfect, they were our families, and we instinctively wanted to start our own.

I was almost thirty and had just moved to a new town with a new job when we decided to start a family. Jan and I just knew that growing our family would be a big part of our lives and our purpose.

In January 1981, we had our first son, Tommy (the one who rarely slept). In April 1983, our second son, John (the fast one), arrived; and then in June 1986, we had our third son, Mike (the steak salesman). We were blessed with three sons, and each one was unique and special to us.

The next twenty years seemed like a blur, but a very good one. Raising our children was exciting and included diapers, learning to walk and talk, kindergarten, Little League, sleepovers, homework, high school sports, and before we knew it, college applications.

Looking back, raising our three sons was clearly the most meaningful thing that Jan and I have ever done in our lives. It was challenging, demanding, eventful, and full of surprises. It was also fun, joyful, and full of laughter. And it was very meaningful.

Starting our family began as a worthy ideal. Once we committed to it, it became our purpose. Pursuing that purpose led to meaning.

WAYS TO INCREASE MEANING

"Align yourself with islands of health and strength. Work with people that want to work with you. Shoot elephants, not squirrels."

—Bob Buford

If you think about it, we all have three choices when it comes to how we spend our time. We can do things that are:

- Meaningful
- Meaning-neutral
- Meaningless

Of course, I don't think anyone really wants to spend too much time on meaningless things; life requires we do some of that anyway. But how do we spend more time on things that have meaning? As I said earlier in this chapter, the most likely places to find meaning are in pursuing *worthy ideals* in the areas of family, career, community, and faith. There are some other key ways to find meaning, too, which I have learned from Dennis Prager, a Jewish philosopher and radio talk-show host. According to Prager, you can also find meaning by doing these things:

- Looking Back.
- Valuing Growth.
- Embracing Differences.
- Doing Hard Things.
- Finding Beauty.
- Finding Wisdom.
- Finding Goodness.

MORE WAYS TO INCREASE MEANING

"Meaning is found on the road to purpose."

—T.W. Lewis

In addition to Prager's powerful ideas on meaning, I have a few more thoughts about where I believe you can find meaning:

- Being your best self. Discovering who you are and what you stand for. Becoming authentic.

- Helping others. Focusing outward more than inward. Serving others with a generous heart.

- Doing things that are estimable. Earning the respect and admiration of others.

- Making and keeping commitments. Saying what you mean. Doing what you say. Not sitting on the fence.

- Never giving up. Persevering in the pursuit of your worthy ideal and pushing through the inevitable hard parts.

USING THE RIGHT WORDS

"Finding meaning requires us to use the right words. Everything can't be 'awesome.'"

—Jeremy Beer

I want to add one final note on an obstacle that may get in the way of finding meaning: the improper use of words themselves. Words are the carriers of meaning. It is in speaking our minds that we often determine just what it is we think. And if we don't use words with precision, we are unlikely to work out the meaning that comes from our experiences, our personal histories, our lives, and our careers.

211

More than 2,500 years ago, the Chinese philosopher Confucius made this point:

> If language is not correct, then what is said is not what is meant; if what is said is not what is meant, then what must be done remains undone; if this remains undone, morals and art will deteriorate; if justice goes astray, the people will stand about in helpless confusion. Hence there must be no arbitrariness in what is said. This matters above everything.

Charles Murray recommends you begin by eliminating the word "like" from your speech—unless you mean to say you approve or desire something. It is a filler verbal tic that distracts and distorts. "Awesome" and "amazing" are two other overused words. In general, avoid the language of inflation both in your speech and in your writing. Calibrate your adjectives to the importance of what you are discussing. Not only will this force you to enrich your vocabulary, but also you will find the world you inhabit begins to become richer, sharper, more detailed, and more complex. And more *meaningful*.

I have three recommendations for putting this piece of advice into practice. First, be sure to proofread and edit every important document you write. Look for areas that are vague or flabby or rely on clichés, and try to rewrite them in more precise terminology. Second, buy and read a good style guide. It is still hard to beat Strunk and White's *The Elements of Style*, now in its fourth edition, which also has the virtue of being short. And third: read, read, read as much as you can—and I mean the really good books. The best way to learn to use words well is by the magic of osmosis. And as a bonus, if you read good books, you'll also find those books to be another satisfying source of meaning.

Meaning isn't something you find; it's something you create. And the best ways to do it include: following worthy ideals, knowing what your values are, learning from the wisdom of others, and being precise—not just in your words but also in your actions. And the byproduct of creating a life of meaning is that you will also find greater happiness.

Chapter 19

EMBRACE WISDOM

"God, grant me the serenity to accept the things I cannot change, the courage to change the things I can, and the wisdom to know the difference."

—Serenity prayer

KNOWLEDGE IS NOT WISDOM

In the late 1990s, I was trying to recruit a person whom I could develop to become my successor at T.W. Lewis Company. I was talking with a recruiter who asked me to describe the characteristics I was looking for in this individual. The first thing that came to mind was, "I want someone who is very intelligent."

"So how do you define intelligence?" he asked.

"I think it is the ability to think fast and process information quickly to get to the right answer," I replied.

"Well, I have a different definition of intelligence: It's the ability to be successful in any situation."

That made a lot of sense to me, because it explained why having a PhD or an Ivy League education doesn't correlate more highly with being successful. It also explained why being a "smart" business executive doesn't necessarily make you a "smart" father or mother. Or why being a "smart" politician doesn't mean you can actually solve problems in the real world.

Shortly after I experienced this change of thinking, I read a book called *The Knowing-Doing Gap* (2000), written by two Stanford professors, Jeffrey Pfeffer and Robert Sutton. These authors explain that having knowledge is not really an advantage until you transform that knowledge into action. *The Knowing-Doing Gap* confronts the myth that people and organizations can compete and succeed by just knowing. Taking action or "doing," not just "smart talk," is the next necessary step in converting knowledge into something that has real value. But before you can take "smart actions" it is necessary to understand "the truth."

FINDING TRUTH

"There is no greatness where there is not simplicity, goodness, and truth."

—Leo Tolstoy

When trying to understand complex topics like truth, it is useful to look them up in the dictionary. For example, *truth* comes from the Latin word *veritas*, which is related to things that are factual, accurate, certain, principled, and ideal. That is quite a high bar. So where can we find truth?

One of my favorite educational nonprofits is Great Hearts Academies, an Arizona-based charter school network whose purpose is to cultivate the hearts and minds of its students in the pursuit of truth, goodness, and beauty. This is how my friend Dr. Rob Jackson, director of the Institute for Classical Education at Great Hearts, describes its process for developing truth seekers:

> From history, we discern patterns of thought and a multitude of questions pouring forth from the self-conscious desire to know one's self: the philosophical quest to understand what is human. *Who am I? Why am I here? What is required of me? How do I live a good life?* These are the questions that have led to our own self-definition as *Homo sapiens*. Translated

from the Latin, we are the "wise ones," with an internal capacity to discern or distinguish among ourselves, others, and the larger world. Yet, how are we to obtain such wisdom?

The only satisfactory answer must be to educate ourselves and our children with the knowledge and experience of the past, building upon the collective wisdom of the human race. But such understanding assumes one key element: Truth. That there is an objective, knowable reality that we can obtain through our abilities to observe, think, imagine, and discern. We seek to know what is real, and we seek to align ourselves with that reality as we best understand it.

But knowing reality is hard, and truth is inconvenient because it requires us to challenge the popular myths of the day. This means that "truth seekers" require courage, strength, and unwavering character and that our society needs more of them.

PRACTICAL WISDOM

"We ask God for strength, and He gives us difficulties to make us strong. We ask Him for wisdom, and He gives us problems."

—Christian saying

Although many smart people (including Plato) thought wisdom was theoretical and abstract, others (including Aristotle) thought differently. Barry Swartz writes in his book *Practical Wisdom* (2010):

Aristotle thought that our fundamental social practices constantly demanded choices—like when to be loyal to a friend, or how to be fair, or how to confront risk, or when and how to be angry—and that making the right choices demanded wisdom. To take the example of anger, the central question for Aristotle was not whether anger was good or bad, or the abstract question about what the nature of the 'good' in fact was. It was the particular and concrete issue of what to do in a particular circumstance: who to be angry at, for how long, in what way, and for what purpose. The wisdom to answer such questions and to act rightly was distinctly practical, not theoretical.

Before you can begin to address questions of wisdom, you first need a moral compass—a belief in some higher order or purpose that provides an understanding of right and wrong, a sense of duty, and a grounding in personal character.

But wisdom, or even "practical wisdom," is not enough unless combined with action. Wisdom in action is called judgment—which is very close to one of the cardinal virtues mentioned in chapter 6, prudence. As mentioned in chapter 12, we can combine these concepts into formulas that look like this:

- Knowledge + Experience + Truth = Wisdom
- Wisdom + Action = Judgment
- Wisdom + Judgment = Prudence

MYTHS PREVENT WISDOM

"It ain't what you don't know that gets you in trouble. It's what you know for sure that just ain't so."

—Mark Twain

Over sixty years ago, in the early 1960s, America was grappling with some difficult issues, including the Vietnam War, widespread student protests, and racial integration. People became angry and were searching for the truth. At the time, President John F. Kennedy said, "The great enemy of truth is very often not the lie—deliberate, contrived, and dishonest—but the myth— persistent, persuasive, and unrealistic."

The need to separate fact from fiction and myth from reality is nothing new. It has been present since the beginning of human time. But just as myth is the enemy of truth, myth is also the enemy of wisdom, because wisdom requires truth.

On a daily basis, you don't have to look beyond the headlines to see how many myths have become embedded in our culture. By ignoring truth, myths can cause people to make bad decisions. In my opinion, here are a few of these myths, along with their opposing realities:

MYTH	REALITY
• Truth is relative.	• Truth is absolute.
• To have a good life, follow your heart.	• To have a good life, follow standards of moral behavior.
• Goodness comes from good intentions.	• Goodness comes from good actions.
• Greatest world threat is climate change.	• Greatest world threat is evil.
• Best solutions for society come from government.	• Best solutions for society come from free markets.

These myths, and many others, prevent wisdom because they don't reflect the true nature of an issue, or root cause of a problem, making it impossible to find a solution.

CODDLING PREVENTS WISDOM

"Knowledge without truth is just data."

—Unknown

In their book *The Coddling of the American Mind*, published in 2018, Greg Lukianoff and Jonathan Haidt expose three major myths widely spread on most college and university campuses in America. Instead of preparing young adults for the opportunities and challenges of life, these popular myths actually make them weaker, less resilient and set them up for failure and unhappiness:

- You are fragile. You can suffer permanent damage from exposure to words or actions with which you disagree.

- Trust your feelings. Whatever you feel in your heart is true, so you, make decisions with emotional versus rational reasoning.

- Life is a battle between good and evil. If someone disagrees with you he is evil, of no value, and his views are not welcomed.

Clearly these myths are powerful and destructive and are a significant contributor to our current social divides.

EMBRACE WISDOM

"When you learn, you know. When you experience, you understand."

—Unknown

Several years ago, I was having a conversation with a group of friends about wisdom, and we decided to do a group exercise around this topic with only two questions:

- "Do you believe wisdom increases with age?" We all said "Yes."

- "What then, specifically, do you know now that you did not know at age thirty?"

After giving the compelling second question much thought, these are my answers:

- Achievement. Everyone enjoys achieving his goals, but not everyone is an achiever. An achiever is someone who is driven to continuously set higher goals and receives irrationnal satisfaction in their accomplishment.

- Adversity. Adversity happens when things don't go your way, when you don't get what you want, or when you encounter real misfortune. How you handle adversity reveals a lot about your character and who you really are. Accepting and overcoming adversity is essential for living a meaningful life because it forges strong values, builds confidence and self-worth, and helps you appreciate all the good you have in your life.

- Alignment. Alignment occurs when a group of people have the same vision, the same goals, the same incentives, and the same values. This can occur with a sports team, a business team, or a family. Only with alignment can groups accomplish great things.

- Authenticity. Everyone wants and deserves to be his or her authentic self, but it is hard to achieve. It takes time, experiences, and challenges to discover who you really are. We are naturally drawn to authentic people, and we're born to be an original, not a copy.

- Balance. Some people believe that living a "balanced life" (one that includes fun, family, community, career, and faith) is the best way to live. But if you are too well-rounded, you're not pointed in any direction. Great things are rarely accomplished by balance. My experience is that you can only be really outstanding at three things. Choose wisely.

- Commitment. Commitment is often overlooked as a key component of success. After you commit to something, good things begin to happen. Because you no longer have the option of quitting, you focus on solutions. Commitment brings out the best in you. And it takes your best to succeed.

- Family. Family is one of the most important things in life. It gives you your most genuine love and your deepest and most meaningful relationships. It provides your sense of belonging, your identity, and your appreciation of history. Your family is forever.

- Improvement. If you could have only one skill for success, it would be the skill to improve. No matter how good you are at anything, you can always get better. Improvement requires a competitive spirit, energy, and persistence. When you focus your improvements on your natural strengths and talents, good things happen.

- Intelligence. Intelligence is widely misunderstood and overrated. It is necessary but not sufficient for success. We are all intelligent about some things and pretty stupid about others. At its essence, intelligence is the ability to succeed in any situation.

- Judgment. Judgment is the ability to understand complex problems and decide what is most important at a given time and place. Not everyone is capable of having good judgment. As an old farmer once said, "Sometimes you need more horse, and sometimes you need more harness." It takes good judgment to know when to do what.

- Leadership. Being a good leader requires only three things: a clear vision, trustworthiness, and compassion. There are many people who are trustworthy and compassionate, but having the skill and courage to define and lead others to a better vision is rare. Leadership is the ability to inspire others to achieve a common goal.

- Passion. Passion is rooted in the Greek word pathos, meaning pain or suffering. It takes a lot of time to find your passion, and passions can change. Passion comes from committing to a worthy cause and suffering the consequences. A lot of young people today are being told to find their passion, but they don't know where to begin. I believe it's better to find your natural strengths (which don't change), and passion will follow.

- People. Every person is unique and mostly good. But we all have flaws. Getting past the flaws and appreciating others for their uniqueness and their goodness is the key to having meaningful relationships with others. In some ways we are all victims of circumstance and deserve compassion.

- Quality. Quality occurs when you satisfy predefined standards and do it right the first time. Getting things right the first time will result in less waste, less frustration, and more satisfaction. Quality is usually better than quantity, and also leads to more satisfaction, meaning, and happiness.

- Security. Security is a myth. It doesn't exist anywhere in nature. With life, there is change. And with change, you lose security. You are better off focusing on learning, growing, adapting, and evolving. Often your biggest mistakes occur when you do nothing.

- Self-Esteem. Self-esteem is the natural result of doing estimable things. It does not come from praise or from reading books on self-esteem. It cannot be given to you by others and can only be earned.

- Talent. Having a natural talent for something is a gift. Like intelligence, it is necessary but not sufficient for success. Hard work always beats talent that doesn't work hard. In general, talent is overrated, but maximizing your natural talent is necessary for success.

- Time. Time is precious and limited, so making the most of your time is the key to becoming your best self. Among the more obvious time-management skills are "doing first things first" and focusing on the important more than the urgent. Wasting time will drain your enthusiasm and opportunities for success. In your career, the worst time-waster is continuing to do the same thing when you are no longer learning and growing.

- Values. Your values are the worthy ideals that matter most to you. A good indication of a person's values is to look at their circumstances or possessions. If a person has a lot of friends, she values friendship. If she has a PhD, she values knowledge. If she has a large bank account, she probably values money. Success is having just enough of all the things that matter most to you.

- Wealth. Wealth can be measured in many ways. You can be wealthy with money, power, and possessions, or you can be wealthy with family, friends, strong faith, good health, a great reputation, and high self-esteem. Being wealthy is having and appreciating all the things that you value.

Wisdom can only be found through the pursuit of knowledge, experience, and truth. Finding knowledge requires effort and stamina, but it doesn't really test your strength or your character. Finding experience, by doing difficult things, requires effort, and it teaches valuable life lessons. Finding truth is, by far, the most difficult. It begins with a solid moral and ethical foundation and becomes a search with tough questions about life and reality. As you search for truth, you find wisdom.

Chapter 20

APPRECIATE HAPPINESS

"The Constitution only guarantees you the right to
pursue happiness. You have to catch it yourself."

—Unknown

HAPPINESS IS A SERIOUS PROBLEM

As I mentioned earlier in this book, when I was about to turn fifty, I had
what you might call a midlife crisis. I had achieved most of my goals, our
sons were leaving home for college, and I was unsure of what to do next.

It was especially hard for Jan and me when we said goodbye to our
first son, Tommy, when we dropped him off at Pepperdine University in
the fall of 1999, just months after my fiftieth birthday. We both cried our
eyes out on the ride back to the L.A. airport, and that sadness continued
for months, as I'm sure it does for many parents at this stage. This period
of time was clearly the least happy one of my life. And I was looking for
answers to the questions that I had about success, purpose, and happiness.

About this time I discovered Dennis Prager, a modern-day philosopher
whom I have already mentioned. I heard about his book *Happiness Is a
Serious Problem* (1998), immediately bought a copy, read it, and learned to
become a much happier person.

First, I learned that our propensity for happiness varies according to
our DNA. Some people are just naturally happier than others. Italians are

happier than the Scottish. Irish are happier than Germans. Extroverts are happier than introverts. You are who you are. Accept it and move on.

Second, I learned that most of our unhappiness is self-inflicted. By seeing what's wrong instead of right, by focusing on ourselves instead of others, by wanting more instead of being grateful, we make ourselves unhappy.

And third, I learned there are many specific ways we can increase (or decrease) our own personal happiness. Based on Prager's book and on my own reflection, I believe there are at least ten specific habits that almost anyone can develop to increase his or her level of happiness.

INCREASING HAPPINESS

TO INCREASE HAPPINESS

- Love others
- Help others
- See the good
- Admire others
- Cultivate wide interests
- Be grateful for what you have
- Be responsible
- Have low expectations
- Seek internal approval
- Face reality

TO REDUCE HAPPINESS

- Be angry at others
- Focus on yourself
- See the bad
- Envy others
- Maintain limited interests
- Always want more
- Be a victim
- Have high expectations
- Seek external approval
- Protect yourself

THE HAPPINESS RECESSION

"Wherever you go, be there."

—Unknown

Several years ago, I heard about a study on happiness in which the researchers selected about 1,000 people to participate. Researchers gave participants a beeper to carry with them at all times, and the beepers went off randomly.

The participants' assignment was to identify what they were doing at that moment and then to score their happiness on a scale of 1 to 10.

The researchers found most people were happier when they were just doing normal activities they enjoyed—like working, exercising, or interacting with family or friends. In other words, they were most happy when they were just living in the present, enjoying where they were and what they were doing.

One of the obvious downsides to having the ubiquitous cell phone is that it makes it so easy to be somewhere else and so hard to just be where you are. And this, along with heavy social media use, is having a major negative impact on our national happiness.

According to recent findings published in *Psychiatric Quarterly* by psychologists Jean Twenge and Keith Campbell, there is a large correlation between heavy social media use and reduced life satisfaction among adolescents. They reported heavy users of digital media were about fifty to 170 percent more likely than light users to be unhappy, suffer from a reduced sense of well-being, or exhibit suicide risk factors.

The addictive qualities of social media are not only a "happiness" problem for young people but are also becoming a major issue for many older adults. The key to managing this, according to writer and philosopher Arthur Brooks, is to make social media a complement, not a substitute, for real human connections. He is clearly right on this.

Another study completed in 2018 by the Institute of Family Studies showed happiness in young adults in America has fallen to a record low, with only 25 percent of adults ages eighteen to thirty-four reporting they were "very happy." Young women were at 28 percent, and young men were at only 22 percent—both numbers down significantly from previously reported levels. To understand the cause of this decline, researchers looked at four factors:

- Marriage. Marriage rates of eighteen to thirty-four-year-olds have declined from 59 percent in 1972 to 28 percent in 2018. Married young adults are 75 percent more likely to report being "very happy" than unmarried ones.

- Faith. The share of young adults who attend religious services more than monthly has fallen since 1972 from 38 percent to 27 percent. Young adults who attend religious services are 40 percent more likely to report being "very happy."

- Friendships. The effects of friendship were less clear than marriage or religion, but young adults who see their friends regularly are about 10 percent more likely to report being "very happy."

- Sex. The share of young adults having sex at least once per week has fallen from 59 percent in 1972 to 49 percent in 2018, with young men falling to 43 percent. The assumption is that this trend is contributing to the decline in "very happy" young adults.

The conclusion of this study on declining happiness is worth noting:

> Young Americans are offsetting some of the lost community and companionship of spouses and churches with closer ties to friends. But those friendships don't give young Americans the sex life that made previous generations happier and may be an indicator of the trouble facing young adults when it comes to love and marriage.

ARISTOTLE ON HAPPINESS

"Happiness is the meaning and the purpose of life, the whole aim and end of human existence."

—Aristotle

Happiness has been studied and pursued for thousands of years, yet it is still hard to define and is often misunderstood. Probably the most profound and lasting theory of happiness was put forth by Aristotle around 350 BC when he concluded that happiness depends on the cultivation of virtue. Today we tend to think of happiness as both short- and long-term life satisfaction, and sometimes even confuse happiness with fun. Although our perceived levels of happiness are constantly changing, our personal "virtue" choices will have long and lasting effects. The key to finding real happiness is to understand its true nature, that we are largely in charge of our own happiness through our thoughts and actions, and that it is really a state of mind.

Any serious discussion of happiness has to include the ideas of Aristotle, whose philosophy of happiness remains profound and relevant after almost 2,400 years. First, Aristotle believed happiness is the ultimate end and purpose of human existence because it is the final end or goal that encompasses the totality of one's life. As our "ultimate end," happiness is self-sufficient, final, and "desirable in itself and never for the sake of something else," he wrote in *Nicomachean Ethics*. Aristotle believed we strive for all the good things in life—like family, friends, success, honor, and wealth—because we think they will make us happy. So happiness is always the final end in itself.

Second, Aristotle believed that happiness depends on the cultivation and exercise of virtue. By virtue, he means the cultivation of moral character and the exercise of this moral character. It is not enough to intend to do something; it is the *exercise* of virtue that creates happiness.

Next, Aristotle said virtue is always the golden mean between two extremes of excess or deficiency. For example, courage is a desirable virtue and is the golden mean between complete fear and absolute recklessness. And justice is the golden mean between "giving or getting too much" and "giving or getting too little."

Further, Aristotle concluded that happiness depends on a broad range of conditions—like health, wealth, knowledge, and friends—"that lead to the perfection of human nature and the enrichment of human life." Unlike pleasure or instant gratification, which can come and go in a matter of hours, happiness cannot be measured until the end of your life when you can weigh all the conditions for a flourishing human existence.

THE HAPPINESS PORTFOLIO

"A joyful life is an individual creation that cannot be copied from a recipe."

—Mihaly Csikszentmihalyi

Fast-forward almost 2,400 years from the days Aristotle created the Lyceum, one of the world's first "think tanks," to the present, and we encounter another think-tank guru—social scientist and philosopher Arthur Brooks. Formerly the longtime president of the American Enterprise Institute, Brooks now focuses on writing and speaking about culture, economics, and politics, but his favorite subject is happiness.

In his book *The Conservative Heart*, published in 2015, Brooks lays out some simple facts about his research on the topic of happiness. First, he explains that three major components control our propensity for being happy:

		Impact on Happiness
• Heredity	DNA, ancestry, personality	48%
• Circumstances	Current events, income, talent, age	40%
• Choices	Decisions, habits, goals	12%
		100%

Brooks describes how to maximize the 12 percent related to your personal choices by focusing on four areas that he calls your happiness portfolio. These are, not surprisingly, faith, family, community, and meaningful work.

Another interesting finding of research on happiness is that age also plays an important role in our level of happiness:

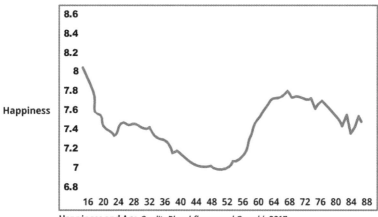

Happiness and Age *Credit: Blanchflower and Oswald, 2017*

Age

To understand this graph is to understand why we look back at high school and college with such fondness and why from ages twenty-two to fifty, we begin to realize that life can be difficult. Then things start to improve— but not until our early fifties.

HAPPINESS CAN BE SIMPLE

As I mentioned in Chapter 1, spending time with my grandparents in Neon, Kentucky gave me a clear picture of how life should be. Looking back, Daddy Buck and Granny had a simple life, but it included all of the most important things like love, family, generosity, decency and faith. Recently, I heard about a new popular song called "Mamaw's House" that had a verse that perfectly described my grandparents' home. My slightly edited version goes like this:

> "If every nightstand had a Bible,
> And every front porch had a swing.
> And every backyard had a garden,
> We wouldn't need another thing."

THE KEY TO HAPPINESS

The key to happiness then, according to Brooks, is to accept the parts of our happiness that we can't control and to take full advantage of the 12 percent that we *can* control. How might we do this? Here are my top ten recommendations for finding your personal happiness:

- Improve your virtues. Grow as a person.
- Be grateful. Count your blessings.
- Improve your relationships. Family and close friends.
- See the good. Nothing is perfect.
- Enjoy your work. Make sure it's meaningful.
- Add variety and fullness.
- Set and achieve meaningful goals. Inspire yourself.
- Lower your expectations. Appreciate where you are.
- Increase your giving. Time, money, and talent.
- Deepen your faith. Believe in something bigger than yourself.

THE ROAD TO HAPPINESS

"Happiness is the natural result of loving other people, being grateful, and living a moral life."

—T.W. Lewis

It is only appropriate that we end this book on a "happy" note with a discussion of happiness, because it is the ultimate achievement of life on this earth. But as we have seen, happiness is highly dependent on other conditions, most of which have been explored within these pages as the building blocks that first need to be in place.

In part II, I discussed what I believe are the foundational requirements for a successful life: personal character, hard work, goal setting, self-awareness, and helping others. In part III, I advanced to the more nuanced areas that will allow you to reach your potential—finding your talent, making good decisions, taking smart risks, keeping your drive alive, and then prudently managing your career.

And finally, in part IV, I have tried to bring some clarity to life's most complex and greatest achievements—success, purpose, meaning, wisdom, and happiness—so that you might better understand and ultimately achieve them.

I trust you will have the opportunity to learn from my life lessons, use some of the models for success and happiness I've presented here, and explore the exercises I've outlined for discovering your values, setting your goals, and finding your purpose. The achievement of a successful and happy life is not an accident. It requires a moral foundation, discipline, and the willingness to reach out of your comfort zone and learn from failure.

My hope is that these final chapters will leave you optimistic about your future and with a mindset that will help you succeed, discover your purpose, find meaning, become wise, and ultimately, be able to say with all honesty that you are happy.

And if you build your life on solid ground, your dots will connect, and success and happiness will surely follow.

Godspeed.

PART V

INSPIRATION FOR THE SOUL

FAVORITE QUOTATIONS

THE POWER OF PERSONAL CHARACTER

"We cannot rise above the limitations of our character."

—John C. Maxwell

"Before we can start winning, we have to stop losing."

—Brian Kelly

"How a person plays the game reveals part of his character. How they lose reveals it all."

—Unknown

"Good character is more to be praised than talent. Most talents are a gift. Good character, by contrast, is not given to us. We have to build it piece by piece."

—John Luther

"What we do to others, we do to ourselves."

—Bryant McGill

"Ability may get you to the top, but it takes character to keep you there."

—John Wooden

"In matters of style, flow like a river. In matters of principle, stand like a rock."

—Thomas Jefferson

"If you have integrity, nothing else matters. If you don't have integrity, nothing else matters."

—Alan Simpson

"Thoughts lead to actions. Actions lead to habits. Habits lead to character. Character leads to destiny."

—James Allen

"When wealth is lost, nothing is lost; when health is lost, something is lost; when character is lost, all is lost."

—Billy Graham

"Character cannot be developed in ease and quiet. Only through experience of trial and suffering can the soul be strengthened, ambition inspired, and success achieved."

—Helen Keller

"Nearly all men can stand adversity, but if you want to test a man's character, give him power."

—Abraham Lincoln

T.W. LEWIS

THE VALUE OF HARD WORK

"There are no elevators to success. You have to take the stairs."

—Zig Ziglar

"The only thing more important than the will to win is the will to prepare to win."

—Vince Lombardi

"My dear, if you would only recognize that life is hard, things would be much easier for you."

—Supreme Court Justice Louis Brandeis to his daughter

"Hard work is where self-worth and self-esteem begin."

—Unknown

"Nothing in the world can take the place of persistence. Talent will not. Genius will not. And education will not. Persistence and determination alone are omnipotent."

—Calvin Coolidge

"Hard work leads to competence. Competence leads to confidence. It takes confidence to succeed and it all starts with hard work."

—Rick Pitino

"Deserve victory. The harder you work, the more you deserve it. The more you deserve it, the more you get it."

—Rick Pitino

"Strength and courage aren't always measured in medals and victories. The strongest people aren't always the people who win, but the people who don't give up when they lose."

—Ashley Hodgeson

"I have not failed. I have just found 10,000 ways that will not work."

—Thomas Edison

"You can win 80% of the time if you just show up, 90% of the time if you show up with a plan, and 100% of the time if you show up with a plan and commit."

—Woody Allen

"The more I want to get something done, the less I call it work."

—Richard Bach

"Don't run out of breath before you win."

—Derek Anderson

"Most people that get ahead do so with the time that others waste."

—Unknown

THE MAGIC OF GOAL SETTING

"If you want your dream to come true, you first have to have a dream."

—T.W. Lewis

"A goal is a dream with a deadline."

—Napoleon Hill

"The value of setting goals is not so much what we achieve,
but what we become in the process."

—Unknown

"If you keep on doing what you've always done, you will keep on getting what
you've always got."

—Unknown

"A man without a goal is like a ship without a rudder."

—Thomas Carlyle

"Begin with the end in mind."

—Stephen Covey

"To avoid criticism: say nothing, do nothing, be nothing."

—Aristotle

"Hope is not a plan."

—Jimmy Dykes

"Get clear. Get Free. Get going!"

—Bob Buford

"The best time to plant a tree was twenty years ago. The second best time is now."

—Chinese proverb

"If the plan doesn't work, change the plan, but never the goal."

—Unknown

"The trouble with not having a goal is that you can spend your life running up
and down the field and never score."

—Bill Copeland

THE BENEFITS OF SELF-AWARENESS

"You were born an original. Don't end up a copy."

—Unknown

"I try my best to be just who I am, but everybody wants you to be just like them."

—Bob Dylan, "Maggie's Farm"

"The unexamined life is not worth living."

—Socrates

"Don't care too much what others think about you, but act in ways that make you proud."

—Dennis Prager

"Know thyself."

—Socrates

"Too many people overvalue what they are not and undervalue what they are."

—Malcolm Forbes

"Between stimulus and response, there is a space."

—Viktor Frankl

"Envy is ignorance. Imitation is suicide."

—Ralph Waldo Emerson

"When I discover who I am, I'll be free."

—Ralph Ellison

"The challenge is not simply to survive. Hell, anyone can do that. It's to survive as yourself, undiminished."

—Elia Kazan

"Be yourself. Everyone else is already taken."

—Unknown

"The curious paradox is that when I accept myself just as I am, then I can change."

—Carl Rogers

THE GOODNESS OF HELPING OTHERS

"If you want to help someone, you tell them the truth. If you want to help yourself, you tell them what they want to hear."

—Thomas Sowell

"Each of us will one day be judged by our standard of life, not by our standard of living; by our measure of giving, not by our measure of wealth; by our simple goodness, not by our seeming greatness."

—William Arthur Ward

"One of life's most important questions is—what am I doing for others?"

—Unknown

"In business and in life, our rewards are directly related to how we serve others."

—Unknown

"Resolve to be tender with the young, compassionate with the aged, sympathetic with the striving, and tolerant of the weak and the wrong. Sometime in your life you will have been all of these."

—Lloyd Shearer

"The opposite of love is not hate. The opposite of love is selfishness."

—Billy Graham

"People don't care about how much you know until they know how much you care."

—Theodore Roosevelt

"One of the kindest things that you can do for yourself is to help others."

—Unknown

"Mankind's greatest need is better understanding of man. All are victims of circumstance, all are under sentence of death and all deserve pity."

—T.G. Lewis

"Be willing to offer others the benefit of the doubt. Perhaps life simply gave them tougher problems than they could solve."

—Unknown

"We make a living by what we get, but we make a life by what we give."

—Winston Churchill

"Helping one person might not change the world, but it could change the world for one person."

—Unknown

FIND YOUR TALENT

"When the student is ready, a teacher will appear."

—Chinese proverb

"The person born with a talent they are meant to use will find their greatest happiness in using it."

—Johann Wolfgang von Goethe

"Hard work beats talent if talent doesn't work hard."

—Sign in University of Kentucky football weight room

"In every person there is a seed of greatness."

—Ezekiel Sanchez

"Don't let anyone stop you. There will be times when you'll be disappointed, but you can't stop. Make yourself the very best that you can make out of what you are. The very best."

—Sadie Alexander

"Adversity is like a strong wind. It tears away from us all but the things that cannot be torn, so that we see ourselves as we really are."

—Arthur Golden

"Life is not the way it's supposed to be. It's the way it is. The way you cope with it is what makes the difference."

—Virginia Satir

"Don't worry about your passion, that changes over time. Find your talent— what you're naturally good at—and work on that. It's your best chance of making a difference in this world."

—T.W. Lewis

"Everyone has talent at twenty-five. The difficulty is to have it at fifty."

—Edgar Degas

"It's easy to make it hard, and it's hard to make it easy."

—Unknown

"Everyone has potential, yet almost no one is reaching it."

—Noah St. John

"Genius is the gold in the mine; talent is the miner that works and brings it out."

—Marguerite Blessington

MAKE GOOD DECISIONS

"When it comes to being successful in life, having good judgment and making good decisions are far more important than just being smart."

—T.W. Lewis

"Life can be hard. And if you make bad decisions, it can be really hard!"

—Unknown

"I am not a product of my circumstances. I am a product of my decisions."

—Stephen Covey

"It is easy to make good decisions when you know your values."

—T.W. Lewis

"Begin challenging your own assumptions. Your assumptions are your windows to the world. Scrub them off every once in a while, or the light won't come through."

—Alan Alda

"There are only two times to make a decision: when you have all the information, and when you have to."

—Unknown

"Fate is the hand of cards we've been dealt. Choice is how we play the hand."

—Marshall Goldsmith

"It is good to understand your problems, but put your energy into the solutions."

—T.W. Lewis

"Moderation is the golden mean between two extremes."

—Aristotle

"A decision is the action a person must take when he has information so incomplete that the answer does not suggest itself."

—Arthur W. Radford

"Two roads diverged in a wood, and I—I took the one less traveled by, and that has made all the difference."

—Robert Frost

"Whenever you see a successful business, someone once made a courageous decision."

—Peter Drucker

TAKE SMART RISKS

"Go out on a limb. That's where the fruit is."

—Unknown

"You will never reach new horizons if you are afraid to lose sight of the shore."

—Unknown

"Security is mostly a superstition. It does not exist in nature."

—Helen Keller

"Twenty years from now you will be more disappointed in the things you didn't do than the things you did."

—Mark Twain

"Don't be afraid to fail. Everyone else has."

—Unknown

"Be fearful when others are greedy, and be greedy when others are fearful."

—Warren Buffett

"If you put all your eggs in one basket, you need to really watch that basket."

—Andrew Carnegie

"Risk and reward go together. If you want the rewards, you will have to take the risks."

—T.W. Lewis

"The problem is that when you don't risk anything, you can risk everything."

—John Spence

"A ship is safe in the harbor, but that is not what ships are made for."

—John A. Shedd

"You miss 100 percent of the shots you don't take."

—Wayne Gretzky

"It is not the critic who counts, not the man who points out how the strong man stumbles or where the doer of deeds could have done them better. The credit belongs to the man who is actually in the arena, whose face is marred by dust and sweat and blood, who strives valiantly, who errs, who comes up short again and again . . . who spends himself in a worthy cause; who, at the best, knows, in the end, the triumph of high achievement; and who at the worst, if he fails, at least fails while daring greatly."

—Theodore Roosevelt

KEEP YOUR DRIVE ALIVE

"Always bear in mind that your own resolution to succeed is more important than any other one thing."

—Abraham Lincoln

"Looking back, we see with great clarity, and what once appeared as difficulties now reveal themselves as blessings."

—Unknown

"In the end, you will be judged not by what you believed, planned or dreamed, but by what you did."

—Unknown

"Motivation is the anticipation of success."

—Unknown

"If I had eight hours to chop down a tree, I would spend six hours sharpening my axe."

—Anonymous Woodsman

"Look in the mirror. That's your competition."

—Eric Thomas

"There are no traffic jams on the extra mile."

—Zig Ziglar

"While you are resting, your competition is getting stronger."

—Sign in a gym

"Things may come to those who wait, but only the things that are left behind by those who hustle."

—Unknown

"Achievement seems to be connected with action. Successful men and women keep moving. They make mistakes, but they don't quit."

—Conrad Hilton

"The man who can drive himself further once the effort gets painful is the man who will win."

—Roger Bannister

"Nobody who ever gave their best regretted it."

—Unknown

MANAGE YOUR CAREER

"Time is free, but it's priceless. You can't own it, but you can use it. You can't keep it, but you can spend it. Once you've lost it, you can't get it back."

—Harvey McKay

"The best way to predict the future is to create it."

—Abraham Lincoln

"Work to become, not to acquire."

—Elbert Hubbard

"Everything will be okay in the end. If it's not okay, it's not the end."

—John Lennon

"To be a leader you have to earn the trust of others. Trust is the natural result of trustworthiness."

—Dennis Prager

"Accomplished people come to wisdom through failure. We get very little wisdom from success."

—Unknown

"If you chase two rabbits, you will catch neither."

—Russian proverb

"The bad news is that time flies. The good news is that you're the pilot."

—Michael Altschuler

"Talent is God-given; be humble. Fame is man-given; be thankful. Conceit is self-given; be careful."

—John Wooden

"It's not what happens to you that is important, it's what you do before it, during it, and after it."

—Alan Weiss

"In life there is not lasting success or failure, only lessons. Life will continue to present you with difficult circumstances until you learn each lesson."

—Unknown

"Choose a job you love, and you will never have to work a day in your life."

—Confucius

ACHIEVE SUCCESS

"If at first you succeed, try something harder."

—John Maxwell

"There are no secrets to success, so don't waste your time looking for them. Success is the result of perfection, hard work, learning from failure and persistence."

—Colin Powell

"Success is the progressive realization of a worthy ideal."

—Earl Nightingale

"The road to success is traveled by those who believe in themselves."

—Unknown

"The only place success comes before work is in the dictionary."

—T.W. Lewis

"I cannot give you the formula for success, but I can give you the formula for failure—try to please everybody."

—Unknown

"Luck is what happens when preparation meets opportunity."

—Seneca

"We like to think of our champions and idols as superheroes who were born different from us. We don't like to think of them as relatively ordinary people who made themselves extraordinary."

—Carol Dweck

"Enthusiasm is common. Endurance is rare."

—Angela Duckworth

"The toughest thing about success is that you've got to keep on being a success."

—Irving Berlin

"Whatever you become, be a good one."

—Unknown

"Nothing worth having comes easy."

—Unknown

DISCOVER PURPOSE

"You can't connect the dots looking forward; you can only connect them looking backwards."

—Steve Jobs

"People plan. God laughs."

—Christian saying

"Don't ask yourself what the world needs. Ask yourself what makes you come alive, and go do that, because what the world needs is people who have come alive."

—Howard Thurman

"The two most important days in your life are the day you are born and the day you find out why."

—Mark Twain

"Resolve to be tender with the young, compassionate with the aged, sympathetic with the striving, and tolerant of the weak and the wrong. Sometime in life you will have been all of these."

—George Washington Carver

"Believe in something big! Your life is worth a noble motive."

—Walter Alexander

"The meaning of life is to find your gift. The purpose of life is to give it away."

—Pablo Picasso

"Your purpose is not determined by yourself, but it is discovered for yourself."

—Unknown

"The purpose of life is to be useful, to be responsible, to be honorable, to help others, to stand for something, to learn, to grow, and strive to be the best that you can be. That is the purpose of life."

—T.W. Lewis

"If you want to know your calling, you need to know your caller."

—Christian saying

"Where there is vision, there is hope."

—Unknown

"Our prime purpose in this life is to help others. And if you can't help them, at least don't hurt them."

—Dalai Lama

CREATE MEANING

"What we obtain too cheap, we esteem too lightly. It is dearness only that gives everything its value."

—Thomas Paine

"Life is a journey of the heart that requires the head. Not the other way around."

—Unknown

"Don't care too much about what others think about you, but act in ways that make you proud."

—Unknown

"It is very difficult to have a meaningful life without meaningful work."

—Jim Collins

"The greatest joy in life is to begin."

—African proverb

"To increase your self-esteem, just start doing more things that are estimable."

—Dennis Prager

"Align yourself with islands of health and strength. Work with people that want to work with you. Shoot elephants, not squirrels."

—Bob Buford

"Meaning is found on the road to purpose."

—T.W. Lewis

"Finding meaning requires us to use the right words. Everything can't be 'awesome.'"

—Jeremy Beer

"You don't have a soul. You are a soul. You have a body."

—C.S. Lewis

"Ever more people today have the means to live, but no meaning to live for."

—Viktor Frankl

"Work gives you meaning and purpose and life is empty without it."

—Stephen Hawking

EMBRACE WISDOM

"God grant me the serenity to accept the things I cannot change, the courage to change the things I can, and the wisdom to know the difference."

—Serenity prayer

"There is no greatness where there is not simplicity, goodness, and truth."

—Leo Tolstoy

"We ask God for strength and He gives us difficulties to make us strong. We ask Him for wisdom and He gives us problems."

—Christian saying

"It ain't what you don't know that gets you in trouble. It is what you know for sure that just ain't so."

—Mark Twain

"The great enemy of truth is very often not the lie—deliberate, contrived and dishonest—but the myth—persistent, persuasive and unrealistic."

—John F. Kennedy

"Knowledge without truth is just data."

—Unknown

"Truth leads to wisdom. Wisdom leads to judgment. Judgment leads to prosperity."

—Unknown

"When you learn, you know. When you experience, you understand."

—Unknown

"On the road of life there are signs. Read them."

—African proverb

"We are all ignorant. Just about different things."

—Mark Twain

"Good judgment comes from experience, and a lot of that comes from bad judgment."

—Will Rogers

"Happy is the one who finds wisdom and the one who gets understanding."

—Proverbs 3:13

APPRECIATE HAPPINESS

"The Constitution only guarantees you the right to pursue happiness. You have to catch it yourself."

—Unknown

"Wherever you go, be there."

—Unknown

"Happiness is the meaning and purpose of life, the whole aim and end of human existence."

—Aristotle

"A joyful life is an individual creation that cannot be copied from a recipe."

—Mihaly Csikszentmihalyi

"Happiness is the natural result of loving other people, being grateful, and living a moral life."

—T.W. Lewis

"Happiness is unrelated to success. Success follows talent, hard work and perseverance. Happiness naturally occurs when you help others and grow as a person."

—Joe Farcht

"Happiness is different than pleasure. It has something to do with struggling, enduring, accomplishing."

—George Sheehan

"Happiness comes indirectly as a dividend. If we make it the object of pursuit, it will lead us on a wild goose chase."

—Unknown

"You will never find happiness until you stop looking for it."

—Unknown

"Happiness is like a butterfly. The more you chase it, the more elusive it becomes."

—Chinese proverb

"The word 'happiness' would lose its meaning if it were not balanced by sadness."

—Carl Jung

"You only need three things to be happy: something to do, someone to love and something to look forward to."

—Ruth J. Lewis

FAVORITE POETRY

INVICTUS

Out of the night that covers me,
Black as the pit from pole to pole,
I thank whatever gods may be
For my unconquerable soul.

In the fell clutch of circumstance
I have not winced nor cried aloud.
But under the bludgeoning of chance
My head is bloody, but unbowed.

Beyond this place of wrath and tears
Looms but the Horror of the shade,
And yet the menace of the years
Finds, and shall find me, unafraid.

It matters not how strait the gate,
How charged with punishments the scroll,
I am the master of my fate:
I am the captain of my soul.

—William Ernest Henley

SOLID GROUND

THE ROAD NOT TAKEN

Two roads diverged in a yellow wood,
And sorry I could not travel both
And be one traveler, long I stood
And looked down one as far as I could
To where it bent in the undergrowth;

Then took the other, as just as fair,
And having perhaps the better claim,
Because it was grassy and wanted wear;
Though as for that the passing there
Had worn them really about the same,

And both that morning equally lay
In leaves no step had trodden black.
Oh, I kept the first for another day!
Yet knowing how way leads on to way,
I doubted if I should ever come back.

I shall be telling this with a sigh
Somewhere ages and ages hence.
Two roads diverged in a wood, and I—
I took the one less traveled by,
And that has made all the difference.

—Robert Frost

T.W. LEWIS

THE MAN IN THE GLASS

When you get what you want in your struggle for self
And the world makes you king for a day,
Just go to the mirror and look at yourself
And see what that man has to say.
For it isn't your father or mother or wife
Whose judgement upon you must pass.
The fellow whose verdict counts most in your life
Is the one staring back from the glass.
Some people might think you're a straight-shooting chum
And call you a wonderful guy,
But the man in the glass says you're only a bum
If you can't look him straight in the eye.
He's the fellow to please—never mind all the rest,
For he's with you clear up to the end.
And you've passed your most dangerous, difficult test
If the man in the glass is your friend.
You may fool the whole world down the pathway of years
And get pats on the back as you pass.
But your final reward will be heartaches and tears
If you've cheated the man in the glass.

—Peter "Dale" Wimbrow Sr.

SOLID GROUND

LUCK

"Do I believe in luck? I should say I do. It's a wonderful force.

I have watched the careers of too many lucky men to doubt its efficacy.

"You see some fellow reach out and grab an opportunity that the other fellow standing around had not realized was there. Having grabbed it, he hangs onto it with a grip that makes the jaws of a bulldog seem like a fairy touch. He calls into play his breadth of vision. He sees the possibility of the situation, has the ambition to desire it, and the courage to tackle it.

"He intensifies his strong points, bolsters his weak ones, cultivates those personal qualities that cause other men to trust him and cooperate with him. He sows the seeds of sunshine, of good cheer, of optimism, of unstinted kindness. He gives freely of what he has, both spiritual and physical things.

"He thinks a little straighter, works a little harder and a little longer; travels on his nerve and enthusiasm; he gives such service as his best efforts permit. He keeps his head cool, his feet warm, his mind busy.
He doesn't worry over trifles.
"He plans his work and then sticks to it, rain or shine. He talks and acts like a winner, for he knows in time he will be one.
And then—luck does all the rest."

—Jack Dionne

T.W. LEWIS

THE UNCONQUERABLE MIND

If you think you are beaten, you are.
If you think you dare not, you don't.
If you like to win, but you think you can't
It is almost certain you won't.

If you think you'll lose, you've lost.
For out of the world we find,
Success begins with a fellow's will.
It's all in the state of mind.

Think big and your deeds will grow.
Think small and you will fall behind.
Think that you can, and you will.
It's all in the state of mind.

If you think you are outclassed, you are.
You've got to think high to rise.
You've got to be sure of yourself before
You can ever win the prize.

Life's battles don't always go
To the stronger or faster man,
But sooner or later the man who wins
Is the man WHO THINKS HE CAN!

—Walter D. Wintle

SOLID GROUND

FINDING TIME

There is so much said of rhythm and reason,
And of fate and time and seasons,
But you must judge who it was that said it,
It is not true just because you read it.
And with this thought you now agree,
You may begin to measure me.

If one would just address himself,
"Am I the cobbler or the elf?
"Am I the one that makes things go?
Or is it a much larger show?"
He may then come to realize
It's to his conscience that he lies.
And if he speaks of his life's sorrows,
Without hope for new tomorrows.
Using words like luck and fate,
He'll never walk among the great.

And many times it has been said,
Of men who now lie cold and dead,
That in their dying breaths have whined,
"Oh, I wish I'd had the time."
To do the more important task,
The thing that I was never asked.
Yet knew that it was charging me,
To set my mind and spirit free.
So once again we hear this plea,
Of men not unlike you and me.
Of men who otherwise had won,
Yet left their tasks still quite undone.
All telling me when I sublime,
God help me say, "I've had the time."

—T.W. Lewis, 1971

255

T.W. LEWIS

DON'T QUIT

When things go wrong, as they sometimes will.

When the road you're trudging seems all uphill,
When the funds are low and the debts are high
And you want to smile, but you have to sigh,
When care is pressing you down a bit,
Rest if you must, but don't you quit.

Life is strange with its twists and turns

As every one of us sometimes learns
And many a failure comes about
When he might have won had he stuck it out;
Don't give up though the pace seems slow—
You may succeed with another blow.

Success is failure turned inside out—

The silver tint in the clouds of doubt,
And you never can tell how close you are,
It may be near when it seems so far;
So stick to the fight when you're hardest hit—
It's when things seem worst that you must not quit.

—John Greenleaf Whittier

SOLID GROUND

IN KENTUCKY

The moonlight falls the softest in Kentucky;
The summer's days come oft'est in Kentucky;
Friendship is the strongest,
Love's fires glow the longest;
Yet, a wrong is always wrongest in Kentucky.

Life's burdens bear the lightest in Kentucky;
The home fires burn the brightest in Kentucky;
While players are the keenest,
Cards come out the meanest,
The pocket empties cleanest in Kentucky.

The bluegrass waves the bluest in Kentucky;
Yet bluebloods are the fewest in Kentucky;
Moonshine is the clearest,
By no means the dearest,
And yet, it acts the queerest, in Kentucky.

The dove's notes are the saddest in Kentucky;
The streams dance on the gladdest in Kentucky;
Hip pockets are the thickest,
Pistol hands the slickest,
The cylinder turns quickest in Kentucky.

Song birds are the sweetest in Kentucky;
The thoroughbreds the fleetest in Kentucky;
Mountains tower proudest,
Thunder peals the loudest,
The landscape is the grandest—
And politics—the damnedest in Kentucky.

—James Hillary Mulligan

FAVORITE STORIES

DANIEL BOONE AND THE BATTLE OF BLUE LICKS

As mentioned in the first chapter of *Solid Ground*, I have learned through ancestral research that I am related to Daniel Boone (1734–1820), the famous woodsman and American folk hero. In fact, two of my 16 second-great-grandfathers are direct descendants of Squire Boone (1696–1765), Daniel's father, and Samuel Boone (1728–1808), one of Daniel's older brothers. I didn't learn this until I was in my early sixties, and with more research I have discovered some interesting history.

Daniel's father, Squire, came to Pennsylvania from Devonshire, England, in 1717, where they met another family, the Bryans, who were from Ireland. When Daniel was 16, in 1750, the Boones and the Bryans moved to Harrisonburg, Virginia, and then one year later they moved to the Yadkin Valley in North Carolina. In 1756, just after serving with the North Carolina militia in the French and Indian War, Daniel married Rebecca Bryan, the sister of William Bryan, one of Daniel's closest friends, and William Bryan married Daniel's sister, Mary.

Daniel Boone first came to Kentucky in 1770, and William Bryan first came in 1775 and brought his family from North Carolina in 1780. Soon thereafter, along with help from Daniel, William Bryan built a small fort with about 40 cabins as a place for new settlers to live in the wilderness and be safe from hostile Indian tribes. It was called "Bryan's Station" and was located just three miles north of what would later become Lexington, Kentucky. Meanwhile, Daniel and his older brother, Samuel (my fifth-great-grandfather), settled about 10 miles away from Bryan's Station in a similar community called "Boone's Station" near future Athens, Kentucky.

With the American Revolutionary War starting in 1776, the British had recruited Indian tribes from as far away as Canada and Michigan to fight and prevent pioneers like Boone, Bryan, and other American settlers from expanding westward. Unfortunately, Daniel and Rebecca lost three of their sons in these wars.

In 1782, as the Revolutionary War was winding down, a group of about 300 hostile Indians, led by British soldiers, quietly surrounded Bryan's Station and waited for an opportunity to attack. The settlers had been under siege for several days and were running out of water since their only well was outside of the fort. Then, a group of six to eight brave women walked out of the fort to the well, as the Indians remained secretly hidden, and gathered enough water to sustain the settlers inside the fort. The bravery of these women under these circumstances became a major frontier news story.

Hearing of this siege from nearby Boone's Station, Daniel and Samuel, along with over 40 militia men, came to Bryan's Station and pursued the Indians about 30 miles north to a place called Blue Licks, where they encountered the Indians in a deadly battle. Many were killed, including Daniel's son, Israel, and the "Battle of Blue Licks" became the last major battle of the Revolutionary War.

One hundred and seventy-nine years later, in 1961, my family moved from Gulf Breeze, Florida, to Lexington. At that time, Lexington had grown to almost 200,000 people and had only three public high schools. The first was named after Henry Clay, the famous Kentucky statesman. The second was named after Lafayette, the French general who helped America win the Revolutionary War. The third high school was named Bryan Station, after the nearby historical site described above. My parents decided to live on the north side of Lexington, so I attended Bryan Station High School.

Over 180 years after the siege of Bryan's Station and the Battle of Blue Licks, I graduated from Bryan Station High School in 1967, not knowing at all how my ancestors were directly involved in the history and naming of my own high school.

THEOPHILUS LEWIS AND THE CHISHOLM TRAIL

Growing up, I had always heard a lot about two of my great-grandfathers from eastern Kentucky. The one on my mother's side was Wilbur Collier (1865–1961), whom I actually got to know. "Grandpa Collier" was Mom's mother's father, who lived to be 96 and spent most of his years in the small town of Neon, Kentucky. Grandpa Collier was a highly respected town leader, businessman, and landowner. He was also a dapper dresser and a real gentleman.

On my dad's side, there was Theophilus Garrard Lewis (1851–1930), who became a well-known lawyer and circuit riding judge in Hyden, Kentucky, which was about 30 miles from Neon. Theophilus was named after his father's best friend, famous Civil War Union General Theophilus Toulmin Garrard. When I first tried to gather more information about Theophilus, all I could find was that he was born in Hyden in 1851 and died in Hyden in 1930. So, I assumed he had spent all of his life in this one small town, just like Grandpa Collier. But later I learned much more about his interesting and adventurous life.

Theo (as he was called) was the tenth and last child of Confederate soldier James "Rebel Jim" Lewis (1812–1869). In 1865 when the Civil War was over and the North had won, Rebel Jim decided to leave the South and move his family to Texas. At that time Theo was only 14 years old, so he went with his mom and dad and a few other siblings in a Conestoga wagon from Hyden, Kentucky, to Weatherford, Texas, just outside of the new town of Fort Worth. We can only imagine how difficult and treacherous this 900-mile journey must have been in 1865.

Once Rebel Jim reached Weatherford, he bought a ranch and some cattle on the Brazos River and young Theophilus quickly became a cowboy. Sadly, Theo's mother died one month after they arrived in 1866, and his father died in 1869, leaving Theo alone at the age of 18. The next year, in 1870, the Kansas Pacific Railroad expanded westward to Kansas City, creating a new and bigger market for Texas ranchers to sell their cattle, as they would be shipped back to the east coast and sold at higher prices. But, to get the cattle to Kansas City, they had to cross three major rivers and travel through over 500 miles of rough Indian territory (exactly like Gus and Woodrow had to do in the movie *Lonesome Dove*!).

Young Theophilus was 19 years old in 1870 when he signed up to drive cattle to Kansas City along what was to become known as the Chisholm Trail. In the years of the cattle drives, cowboys drove large herds from ranches across Texas to Red River Station and then north to Kansas City along this trail. From 1870 to 1880, it was estimated that more than 5 million head of cattle traveled the Chrisholm Trail from Texas to Kansas. After a few years of driving cattle, Theo wisely decided it was time to get serious about his future. He then moved back to Kentucky, went to a small law school in Louisville, and learned to become a lawyer. In 1879 he married his first cousin, Drucilla Lewis, and they had three children. The oldest of these was William Henry Lewis, my grandfather.

As Theo's career progressed, he traveled by horseback for many years as a circuit riding judge throughout Kentucky and then later settled down in his hometown of Hyden as a judge and prominent attorney. By 1900, he had become a large landowner and was actively involved in the booming timber and coal businesses in eastern Kentucky. Years later, Theo and his double first cousin, Lou Lewis were both featured as early circuit riding judges in a book named *They Have Topped the Mountain*, which was published in 1960.

Theophilus Garrard Lewis died on February 21, 1930, at the age of 78 in the same small town where he was born. But his life story was far more interesting and adventurous than you would know from only reading the dates and towns on his tombstone.

FAVORITE BOOKS

- *The Bible*
- *Nichomachian Ethics* (350 BC) by Aristotle
- *As a Man Thinketh* (1903) by James Allen
- *How to Win Friends and Influence People* (1936) by Dale Carnegie
- *The Strangest Secret* (1957) by Earl Nightingale
- *Man's Search for Meaning* (1959) by Viktor Frankl
- *The Precious Present* (1981) by Spencer Johnson
- *Seven Habits of Highly Effective People* (1989) by Stephen Covey
- *Life's Greatest Lessons* (1992) by Hal Urban
- *Happiness Is a Serious Problem* (1998) by Dennis Prager
- *Winning* (2005) by Jack Welch
- *Outliers* (2008) by Malcolm Gladwell
- *Talent Is Overrated* (2008) by Geoff Colvin
- *The Defining Decade* (2012) by Meg Jay
- *The Only Way to Win* (2012) by Jim Loehr
- *Still the Best Hope* (2012) by Dennis Prager
- *The Curmudgeon's Guide* (2014) by Charles Murray
- *12 Rules for Life* (2018) by Jordan Petersen
- *Letter to the American Church* (2022) by Eric Metaxes
- *The Anxious Generation* (2024) by Jonathan Haidt

ABOUT THE AUTHOR

 Tom Lewis is an award-winning business-man, entrepreneur, and philanthropist based in Phoenix, Arizona. Founded in 1991, T.W. Lewis Company built over 5,000 homes in metro Phoenix and is best known for its outstanding quality and customer service in the homebuilding industry. Among its numerous industry awards are the America's Best Builder Award in 1998 and the National Housing Quality Gold Award in 2009. In 2013 Tom received a Lifetime Achievement Award from Professional Builder Magazine and the National Housing Quality Award Committee and was named the first inductee into the National Housing Quality Hall of Fame.

In 2000, Tom and his wife, Jan, formed T.W. Lewis Foundation that supports higher education, children and families in need, Christian education, and a variety of national non-profit organizations that strengthen America. T.W. Lewis Foundation has provided over 200 college scholarships to outstanding students to attend some of America's best universities. In 2015, Tom and Jan founded the Lewis Honors College at the University of Kentucky.